# SOCIAL CAPITAL

## IN

# HEALTHCARE

# SOCIAL CAPITAL

# IN

# HEALTHCARE

## HOW **TRUST** AND **TEAMWORK** DRIVE
## ORGANIZATIONAL EXCELLENCE

# THOMAS H. LEE, MD
### CHIEF MEDICAL OFFICER, PRESS GANEY
### AND EDITOR-IN-CHIEF, NEJM CATALYST

WILEY

Published by John Wiley & Sons, Inc., Hoboken, New Jersey.
Published simultaneously in Canada.

For general information on our other products and services or for technical support, please contact our Customer Care Department within the United States at (800) 762-2974, outside the United States at (317) 572-3993 or fax (317) 572-4002.

Wiley also publishes its books in a variety of electronic formats. Some content that appears in print may not be available in electronic formats. For more information about Wiley products, visit our web site at www.wiley.com.

*Library of Congress Cataloging-in-Publication Data is Available:*

ISBN: 9781394312658 (cloth)
ISBN: 9781394312665 (ePub)
ISBN: 9781394312672 (ePDF)

Cover Design: Wiley
Cover Image: © Moyo Studio/Getty Images
Author Photo: © Press Ganey

SKY10092893_120524

*To Michael E. Porter, PhD, MBA*

*Bishop William Lawrence University Professor*

*Harvard Business School*

*Who taught me and so many others to focus on measuring what matters and organize around its improvement—the ideas at the core of this book.*

# Contents

# *Preface*

Creating social capital is something that comes naturally to most people – especially people who are drawn to the good work of healthcare. Social capital is generated by creating social networks and using them to improve what we do. We tend to enjoy building connections with others in our personal and professional lives. We like to strengthen those connections, too. We value being able to work with people we like and trust.

But *building* social capital so that our organizations do more for our patients with high reliability and earn the loyalty of our colleagues – now, that takes work. It takes discipline. It means building real connections with everyone on the team. It means making sure everyone *knows* that they are on a team. It means creating a culture in which everyone – patients and colleagues – feels respected.

It means building connections *across* teams and *across* organizations. It means using those connections to spread information quickly and reliably, so we can respond to the challenges of the moment and the challenges of our times. It means creating a context in which people trust each other because they understand what it takes to be trustworthy.

Building social capital is difficult work – but it is the best work. It is the kind of work that causes you to smile gently every now and then as you drive home after a good day. Most of us feel that this is the kind of work we would do without the need for compensation. In fact, research shows that managers who are better at building social capital are valued more highly by their organizations and get promoted more quickly.

This book is written to help managers and leaders thrive by enhancing their ability to create social capital for their organizations. I don't think readers will find any of the recommendations controversial; after all, who can be against building connections among people and putting them to good use? But I hope the framing of these recommendations will help managers and leaders focus on the steps that build social capital.

I write this fully aware that "focusing" is not easy in healthcare even when the goal has obvious importance, like the building of social capital. There are so many signals coming in from so many directions in healthcare all the time, and every one of them feels like a crisis. There are health crises, like the COVID-19 pandemic. There are social crises that result from bias and inequity. There are financial crises due to the high costs of healthcare. And, of course, for each individual patient, there are their own medical crises that must be addressed with urgency.

In healthcare, we are better wired for responding to urgency than focusing on steps to build capital of any kind – financial or social. However, healthcare's current challenges demonstrate that working hard in response to crises is not enough. We need to be able to step back and understand what types of organizational changes will enable us to deliver better care and then implement them with high reliability.

My personal education on the types of organizational changes that are essential to building social capital began one June day in 2006, when I had my first real interaction with Michael E. Porter, a professor from Harvard Business School who would subsequently become my colleague, coauthor, and good friend. Porter was already widely known as one of the most powerful thinkers about business strategy, and he had just published *Redefining Health Care* – a book (written with Elizabeth Teisberg) that overnight had found a place on virtually every healthcare leader's bookshelf (Porter and Teisberg 2006).

I had invited Porter to lunch with me and my boss, Jim Mongan, CEO of what was then Partners Healthcare System (now MassGeneral Brigham) because he posed a problem. My job at that time was network president for Partners. I was responsible for building the network of physicians and hospitals around Massachusetts General Hospital and Brigham and Women's Hospital and improving their quality and efficiency. The goals of this work were idealistic, but they were also strategic. We were negotiating contracts with payers as an integrated delivery system, and we were getting compensated at higher levels than other providers because, in theory, the whole of our system was greater than the sum of its parts.

We were successful enough in those contract negotiations that we were attracting criticism from health insurance companies, other providers, and some government officials. Then, in the spring of 2006, we heard that Porter was saying in public remarks that Partners was not really an integrated delivery system. A powerful voice had joined the chorus of our critics.

"That's not good," Mongan said to me. "Ask him if he would come over so we can tell him all the things we are doing to integrate our care." I reached out to Porter and invited him to lunch; he agreed, and a few weeks later, I found myself sitting with Mongan across the table from arguably the most respected expert on business strategy in the world.

I had printed out PowerPoints showing how we were implementing electronic health records (EHRs) across our system. We were not only making an EHR available, but we required physicians to adopt it. We were the first network in the country to tell doctors that if they didn't adopt an EHR, we would exclude them from our network and our contracts. (We ultimately excluded about 35 doctors who refused to come along; it was not pleasant.)

Porter paid close attention, writing notes on his yellow pad. He nodded when I described the decision support that we were integrating into our EHR to help doctors make safer and more efficient choices. I paused to give him a chance to compliment us on our work.

"That's all very lovely," he said. This was the moment when I learned that if you hear the word "lovely" in a business context, you are not going to like what is coming next. He continued, "But it's not the same thing as organizing around the needs of patients."

My heart sank, because I knew immediately that he was right. We were working hard to make doctors faster, safer, and even more efficient at doing what doctors do, but we had not really done much to reorganize what they did.

Mongan made some hand motions to tell me to keep going. I went to the pages in the PowerPoint presentation that described the financial incentives we had created to reward physicians who improved on their quality metrics and/or decreased their spending for the overall population.

Again, Porter nodded. And, again, he said, "Yes, that's all very good. But it's not the same as organizing around the needs of patients."

After a few more minutes of playing defense, I surrendered. I said, "Michael, if you were us, what would you do?"

"I would make Partners the world's leaders in measuring what matters to patients," he said. "Capture those data and put them in front of your doctors. You are good people and you are smart people. You will respond and you will figure out how to make care better. But if you don't measure what matters to patients, you can't."

I was taking notes and wrote, "Measure what . . . " in my notebook, but then stopped. Porter was sitting only a few feet away across the narrow table and could see what I wrote. I thought that he must be wondering, "What are they paying this guy for if he has to write down that they should measure what matters to patients?"

But his suggestion was a big one. He was recommending that Partners and the rest of healthcare organize around a new focus – improving what matters to patients. We had never been against that goal, of course. But Porter was suggesting that we make it our explicit top priority and organize ourselves accordingly.

"If you want to discuss what it means to go down this road, come on over and we can continue the conversation," he said.

And the very next day, I did.

Years later, when Porter and I were making our way through a crowd entering Fenway Park for a Red Sox game, I recalled that afternoon when we had met – and told him that after he left, several of my colleagues were waiting in a conference room to hear what had happened during the meeting with him. I told them, "He said we should measure what matters to patients." They had all bent over and furiously written in their notebooks, "Measure what matters to patients."

Porter laughed. "Don't feel bad about writing that down," he said. "This is what happens in every organization among people doing *real* work. They get so close to it that they can lose sight of the big picture.

"I have a great job," he continued. "I come in and say the obvious thing. And then I go away, hoping that I helped them focus on that obvious stuff."

With the benefit of time, I now understand that focusing on the obvious things – the true top priorities – is one of the most important lessons that I learned from Porter. Another is the importance of *organizing* around the true top priorities. (I did get the chance to watch with amusement when Porter said to a classroom full of senior healthcare executives at a Harvard Business School course: "How you are organized really matters." From my place in the back row, it looked like every one of them were writing in their notebooks, "How you are organized really matters. . . .")

One of the key concepts that Porter brought to management was value chain analysis – identifying the key activities necessary to create value for your customer and giving those activities intense attention. Porter and I would later write about how value chain thinking helps managers give *less* attention to the issues that *don't* create value for their customers, such as internal politics, so they can focus on what *does*. And we would write about a strategic framework for creating value in healthcare, which I discuss later in this book.

In hindsight, I realize that he was taking me down a road to focusing on the creation of social capital. That road took me to my work as the chief medical officer of Press Ganey, and it took me to my role as the editor-in-chief of *NEJM Catalyst*, a publication we started to accelerate progress toward a high-value healthcare system. (Porter co-chaired the Editorial Board with me as we got it off the ground.)

And now that road has taken me to writing this book, which I hope will integrate the most important lessons that I have learned from colleagues inside and outside healthcare and from my ongoing work as a practicing physician. I feel fortunate to be functioning as a broker of the flow of information and insights from them to you. And one of those insights is that improvement is a social function.

# Introduction

"I'm a chief officer for social capital." That's the mindset I hope this book will instill in every reader. Being a CO for social capital means readers will approach building social capital in their part of the organization with the same intensity and discipline as their CFO brings to managing the organization's financial capital. Moreover, the evolution of managers of healthcare delivery into COs for social capital is critical to the effectiveness, viability, and success of their organizations.

The term *social capital* refers to the accumulation of resources people develop by connecting with one another. Building social capital is just as important as building financial capital – in fact, possibly more so. Just as financial capital is the money that enables organizations to do things they otherwise could not do, human capital is the people who enable organizations to do things they otherwise could not do. Social capital is how those people interact with each other and their infrastructure.

Organizations can borrow money from the outside. They can hire temporary help from agencies. But nothing can create trust, teamwork, and high reliability for organizations except the people within the organization.

At first glance, social capital may seem fuzzy – not something as real as money. After all, some of the currencies of social capital – terms like *connectedness*, *respect*, and *trust* – are often tossed around as aspirational flourishes, when in fact they are assets to be managed.

But anyone who delivers patient care knows that excellence is impossible without social capital. At the front lines, how you are organized *really* does matter. Teamwork *really* does matter. And you can't have good teams without team members who trust each other and who share values like respect, communication, and coordination.

Social capital is analogous to financial capital in important ways. Financial capital, more than its year-to-year operating margin, determines an organization's ability to construct new buildings, for example, or individuals' ability to pay tuitions or make large purchases. For individuals, wealth is driven more by their accumulated financial capital than their annual salaries. Like financial capital, social capital takes time to build, but the investment is worth the payoff.

As I argue in this book, the more social capital a healthcare organization accumulates, the stronger it becomes. Information flows throughout and among all levels of the organization. Employees – from support staff to caregivers to executives – become more engaged in their work and aligned with the organization's mission. Productivity increases, and the organization is able to become a "high reliability organization" – a designation reserved for "organizations that operate in complex, high-hazard domains for extended periods without serious accidents or catastrophic failures" (Agency for Healthcare Research and Quality 2019).

If financial capital is the key determinant of wealth, social capital is the key determinant of *resilience* – the ability to withstand crises and recover quickly. Without resilience, healthcare organizations can founder and fail. Consider the harrowing story of Memorial Hospital in New Orleans, a safety-net provider. When Hurricane Katrina struck in August 2005, unsafe conditions within the hospital and lack of an effective protocol to evacuate patients and staff resulted in the deaths of 45 patients. Ultimately, the hospital was forced to close.

In contrast, resilience stemming from social capital built up over years enabled Brigham and Women's Hospital to handle the tide of injured survivors streaming into the Emergency Department following the Boston Marathon Bombing of 2013. Over a few hours, 39 severely injured survivors poured into the Brigham's Emergency Department. Not one person died. The Emergency Department teams credited their success on training modified after the Navy Seal experiences of one of its leaders.

A few paragraphs from an extraordinary article in the *New England Journal of Medicine* described that day in detail:

> For the next few hours, survivors continued to arrive. They kept coming.

Overall, we treated 39 survivors, ranging in age from 16 to 65 years. Nine patients required emergency operative intervention for open fractures, amputations, devascularized limbs, burns, and shrapnel removal. Many required second, third, and even fourth operations to wash out debris, remove dead tissue, stabilize fractures, and perform myocutaneous flap replacements of missing tissue. Some required vascular reconstructions, placement of external fixators, and fasciotomies of the legs.

These complex procedures took careful planning and coordination across all surgical disciplines. We also treated patients with less severe injuries, such as ear barotrauma and shallow shrapnel penetrations. These patients were invariably more concerned for the other victims than they were for themselves.

In these extraordinary circumstances, successful care came from colleagues working alongside familiar teammates, performing familiar tasks. When challenged, each team performed as if the situation were routine. In Boston, we fight like we train (Goralnick and Gates 2013, p. 1960).

The Brigham's response to the bombing didn't end after the injured were treated. In the ensuing week, the hospital faced numerous other challenges. Local police and federal agents stormed into the corridors as a "person of interest" in the bombing was treated for injuries. Loved ones of the seriously injured were accommodated as guests in empty patient rooms. Boston mayor Tom Menino, who was recovering from surgery in the hospital at the time of the bombing, set up a de facto City Hall in his room. First Lady Michelle Obama visited the injured, necessitating the engineering of a safe, private passageway for her entrance and exit. The communications team created a 24/7 media "command central" to update the press.

The weeklong crisis required an extra effort from every department of the hospital – from food services and housekeeping to caregivers to executive officers. In acknowledgment, a "BWH Strong" button was minted, and by the end of April, almost everyone who walked the halls was wearing one. The hospital also reconfigured an early May celebration – originally planned as a donor apprecia-tion event associated with the hospital's centennial – into a celebration honoring those who helped save lives and supported each other during this difficult time.

How the Brigham responded to the Boston Marathon bomb-ing is just one of many examples of how organizations with strong financial capital have weathered storms – sometimes literally. For example, Houston Methodist began a long-term program to adopt the principles of a high-reliability organi-zation in order to improve quality and safety early in this century. Its leaders ultimately credited this work as helping it respond to a series of disasters in recent years, including trop-ical storms and the COVID-19 pandemic (Phillips et al. 2021).

I acknowledge that some readers may have a negative reac-tion to the phrase *social capital*, because we haven't found a "conversion factor" to equate social good to financial interactions. I also sense the growing concern that the "financialization" of healthcare and the obsession with maximizing financial returns can lead to harm for patients and burnout among the people delivering healthcare – in effect eroding social capital.

However, financial concerns have *always* been important in healthcare, and likely always will be. Today, financial concerns are being amplified by medical progress and its associated costs, the rapid flow of information and money, and the evolution of organizations that can capitalize on those flows. To suggest that financialization can be stopped or reversed is not realistic.

What *is* realistic is to create an additional focus on social capital and to have this focus compete with financial concerns for the attention of leaders and boards of directors. Social capital enables organizations to do more and be better without adding more costs or people. Building social capital does require real work, however – the work of learning how to collaborate and thus to make the whole greater than the sum of its individual parts. It requires leadership at the top of organizations and disciplined management at the front lines.

The work is difficult. It is, in many ways, swimming against the tide of worrisome societal trends, like the erosion of trust and increasingly widespread social isolation. A vast array of data documenting these trends is summarized in Surgeon General Vivek Murthy's advisory from 2023, *Our Epidemic of Loneliness and Isolation*. Polls from the 1970s showed that about 45% of Americans felt that they could reliably trust other Americans; that proportion was just 30% in 2016. Other data show that the amount of time that people spend engaged with friends socially decreased from about 60 minutes per day in 2003 to 20 minutes per day in 2016, with the biggest decline in young people ages 15 to 24. This decline has been accompanied by a rise in mental health problems, and many experts, including Surgeon General Murthy, believe that online social network apps are worsening social capital, not building it.

Healthcare leaders talk more about finances than "softer" issues like the social capital of their workforce because money feels more tangible. But, as difficult as it may be to build social capital in this context, most leaders know that social capital leads to business success – especially in a field like healthcare, where teamwork is so critical and patients' needs are so variable.

An explicit goal of this book is to make social capital more tangible for managers in healthcare – to describe what social capital is and why it is important; to show how it is built and measured; to give case studies of examples of healthcare organizations that are building social capital; and to provide a playbook for how managers can approach social capital like their CFOs approach financial capital – by measuring it, analyzing the data, prioritizing opportunities for increasing it, making plans, and assessing progress on those plans.

This kind of work already goes on in most healthcare organizations, but the goal of this book is to make that work clearer and more effective.

# Chapter 1

# A Primer on Social Capital

L et's start by defining what we mean by *capital*. A simple description is "anything that confers value or benefit to its owners" (Hargrave 2024). This definition makes one thing clear – capital is good to have, and having more is better than having less. Capital gives its owners an advantage – an edge in comparison not only with their competitors but also with their current selves. In other words, capital enables organizations to improve.

Differences in how organizations perform can often be explained by their access to various types of capital. If they have more *financial capital* (money), they can build new facilities. If they have more *human capital* (capable employees), they can start new programs and adequately staff existing ones to meet the needs of their customers. If they have more social capital, they can do everything more creatively and efficiently. If financial capital and human capital determine what an organization has the potential to do, social capital enables the organization to fulfill that potential.

Five books have been particularly influential in shaping my appreciation of social capital and providing clarity on the steps that can be taken to build it in healthcare. All five are written for general audiences, but their insights are highly relevant to the work of healthcare:

1. *Bowling Alone*, by Robert D. Putnam (2020)
2. *Brokerage and Closure: An Introduction to Social Capital*, by Ronald S. Burt (2005)
3. *Connected*, by Nicholas A. Christakis and James H. Fowler (2009)
4. *Teaming*, by Amy C. Edmondson (2012)
5. *Team of Teams*, by General Stanley McChrystal et al. (2015)

In aggregate, these books describe:

- The essential elements of social capital – reciprocity and trust
- Two types of connections that form the scaffolding of social capital – bonding and bridging
- The function of social networks formed by bonding and bridging connections
- The importance of teamwork – from teams formed on the fly to teams of teams

Before going into these interrelated topics, we begin with some general insights about the nature of social capital and why it has emerged as an important topic in recent years.

## Social Capital's Arrival

The concept of social capital was introduced to many in the year 2000 with the publication of the first edition of

*Bowling Alone* by Robert Putnam. The book's title reflects Putnam's observation that "[g]iven population growth, more Americans are bowling than ever before, but *league* bowling has plummeted" (Putnam 2020, p. 112).

In dozens of examples, Putnam shows that Americans are less connected in ways that once gave meaning to the term *social fabric*. Bridge clubs had broken up and attendance at Parent-Teacher Associations was down. At Tewksbury Memorial High School near Boston, "forty brand-new royal blue uniforms newly purchased for the marching band remained in storage, since only four students signed up to play" (Putnam 2020, p. 16). Two decades before, there had been 80 members in the band, but membership had been dropping ever since. The downward trend of social involvement has only increased since the turn of the 21st century. For example, church membership, which stood at 70% in 1970 (Jones 2021), dropped below 50% in Gallup surveys for the first time in 2020.

Putnam argued that these changes in civic and social life in America were important and were eroding what he called "social capital." He was not the first social scientist to use this term (Bourdieu 1986, pp. 241–258), but it was novel enough at the time that he put the term in quotation marks the first time he used it. Putnam went on to say that the "core idea of social capital theory is that social networks have value[;] . . . social contacts affect the productivity of individuals and groups" (2020, p. 19).

Putnam defined *social capital* as "social networks and the norms of reciprocity and trustworthiness that arise from

**11**

them" (ibid.), which, in a community or an organization, translate into ways in which people relate to each other and work together. These shared norms, values, and understandings facilitate cooperation in healthcare – within teams, between different groups in an organization, and between the organization and other stakeholder organizations. Social capital can also influence interactions between staff and patients and their families.

*Bowling Alone* attracted wide attention, including among many in healthcare, because it arrived as people working in the field were beginning to realize that their work had become . . . lonely. Because of medical progress, there were more people working in healthcare organizations than ever before, but the paradoxical effect was that people felt isolated.

The use of electronic medical records was becoming mandatory at this time. Activities that were once performed in groups, like going down to radiology to look at x-rays together, were increasingly replaced by individual interactions at computer terminals. Even when clinicians *did* round on patients together, they were looking at computer screens more than at patients or each other.

The changes were not just at the bedside. In an article I published in the *New England Journal of Medicine,* "Quiet in the Library," I made a number of observations about my medical school library:

> The library at my medical school has never been a better place to work. The journals are shelved in perfect order. The copying machines have no lines.

Quiet, comfortable places in which to read are plentiful. The reason: hardly anyone goes there anymore.

Only a few years ago, this library was noisy, chaotic, and often frustrating – but it was full. For the researchers, medical students, and physicians who once haunted the stacks, the need for access to information has only intensified. But an explosion of knowledge, combined with the emergence of the Internet as the ideal searching tool, is transforming medicine, with implications reaching far beyond the library walls (Lee 2005, p. 1068).

My article continued: "Memorization is a solitary activity; learning how to think when confronted with uncertainty is not." That kind of work – *thinking*, as opposed to *reacting* – is often essential for truly excellent patient care. Reacting dominates one's time when sitting at a computer terminal. Thinking goes better when people are working and learning together.

I know the following sounds idealistic, but it happens to be true: Well-functioning groups are always smarter than the smartest individual within them. We all have blind spots. We all make mistakes. If people within a group are really interacting, they catch each other's mistakes and they point out each other's blind spots.

But that requires real connections among them.

# The Currencies of Social Capital: Reciprocity and Trust

Robert Putnam's book focused on the connections individuals have with their communities, while Ronald Burt's book, *Brokerage and Closure*, is more directly relevant to organizations seeking to improve their performance. But both books describe elements of connections that managers in any type of organization will recognize as important in their professional worlds – reciprocity and trust. Just as dollars and euros are the currencies of financial capital, reciprocity and trust are the currencies of social capital.

## Reciprocity

Putnam expresses general reciprocity as "I'll do this for you without expecting anything specific back from you, in the confident expectation that someone else will do something for me down the road" (2020, p. 21).

In retrospect, I realize that he might well have been paraphrasing the message I received a few days after I arrived at Brigham and Women's Hospital to start my medical internship. I told my senior resident that another intern had asked me to cover his patients for two hours while he dashed out to finalize his apartment rental; I wanted to be sure it was OK. My resident said, "Sure." And then he looked up from the record he was reviewing and added, "You never say 'no' to a fellow intern here."

I was taken aback. It was a casual remark, but I knew that he was asserting something important about our group of 24 interns – and I liked it. I knew that I would never ask anything of my fellow interns that I didn't really need. But, if I had to ask, it was great to know that they would almost surely say "yes."

With time and experience, I came to understand that my resident was helping create a type of social capital gold – a group norm in which colleagues say "yes" without having to know the details. When you have strong bonds within the group, you don't have to size up the situation before you agree to a request. Teams work better and people are happier when that type of social capital exists.

Not every person in our internship group embraced the norm of saying yes without having to know the details, but it was true for most of us right from the start, and more adopted it as the year went on. That improvement over time highlights an important difference between financial and social capital. When you spend financial capital, you have less of it. But social capital has reinforcing effects and virtuous cycles; the more you create and put to the test, the more you get. Trust grows when trust passes tests. Someone says "yes" to you when you need help, and you say "yes" when you are asked to do the same.

Reciprocity is qualitatively different from doing something for altruistic reasons or doing something because it is in your personal self-interest and you are expecting to be paid back by the other party. You do what you are supposed to do because the members of the group share long-term mutual interests, and a group norm like never saying no to each other leads to acts that collectively benefit everyone in the group.

Reciprocity isn't restricted to small groups like the 24 people who were interns with me. For example, in some communities, there is a strong social norm that "we take care of our own," and when someone is discharged from the hospital, their neighbors take turns bringing food and helping out in other ways. The result is that often the use of skilled nursing facilities and rehabilitation hospitals is much lower in these communities.

Reciprocity doesn't just happen out of the kindness of people's hearts. Reciprocity usually becomes a norm when there is a sense that there are consequences if one does not participate. Those consequences tend to be social, not financial. If you don't embrace the norm, you risk being ostracized.

One example from healthcare is the expectation among clinicians at the Mayo Clinic that you always answer a page from another clinician immediately. It can be a doctor calling a doctor to share worrisome news, or a nurse calling a physician to say a patient had developed a fever and was delirious. The issue doesn't matter; if you are a clinician being paged by another clinician, you answer right away. You don't finish driving to where you are going; you pull off the road. You don't finish a conversation, even with a patient; you excuse yourself and answer the page.

As a result, clinicians talk to each other on the phone rather than just through the electronic medical record or emails. Radiologists don't recommend additional tests at the end of their readings; they simply page the clinician who ordered the test. They feel like team members even when they don't see each other often or at all.

This isn't the way it is at most organizations in healthcare. Much more common are cultures in which physicians answer pages if and when they choose to. And because no one knows when a page will be answered, clinicians often don't bother. They send their information or their requests by emails that sometimes get read at midnight or the next day.

It's obviously better for patient care if clinicians talk to each other right away, but I was skeptical when I first heard about the Mayo immediate-answer norm. Nevertheless, I found it to be true during my first visit to the Mayo Clinic in 2015. It occurred to me that I wanted everyone else to drop what they were doing and answer me right away when I paged them, but I didn't particularly want to do that myself (the opposite of reciprocity).

When I asked doctors at the Mayo Clinic why they reliably did what they are supposed to do and answered their pages right away, they looked at me like I was asking a dumb question. I pushed ahead, and said, "Well, what would happen if you *didn't* answer your page immediately?" I felt like the Devil, tempting them with the possibility of them doing something bad.

One said, "The earth would open, and you would be swallowed up and disappear." Another said, "You would be put outside in the winter cold, and you would die." A third said something slightly less colorful but still compelling: "You just don't want people to say that you are the kind of person who doesn't answer his page."

Clinicians at Mayo know that if they answer their colleagues' pages right away, *their* pages will get answered right away too. To bring the concept of reciprocity to life, Putnam cites two quotes: one from Yogi Berra – "If you don't go to somebody's funeral, they won't come to yours" – and another associated with the Gold Beach, Oregon, Volunteer Fire Department – "Come to our [fundraising] breakfast; we'll come to your fire (Putnam 2020, p. 20)."

The firefighters were not really suggesting that they would come to your fire only if you came to their fundraising breakfast. Instead, they were reminding others that they could be trusted to come fight fires wherever and whenever they occurred. It was reasonable for them to therefore trust that the town's citizens would turn out for their fundraising breakfast. It was a gentle reminder that reciprocity should characterize their relationships.

Healthcare needs that same reciprocity dynamic between caregivers and patients and among caregivers themselves. Taking care of patients is every bit as unpredictable as firefighting, and patients need to be able to trust that healthcare personnel will respond when the need arises. An effective response to patients' needs usually requires more than the efforts of one individual. Teams must respond with caregivers who can rely on each other to do whatever it takes to meet the needs of patients and each other.

## Trust

Both Putnam and Burt plunge deeply into the topic of trust. Putnam points out that groups characterized by

**18**

trustworthiness work more efficiently for the same reasons that money makes transactions more efficient than barter. Imagine having to consider whether a dozen eggs is a reasonable trade for a hammer. Or imagine working with colleagues who say "Let me think this over" every time you ask them to do something. Most managers are all too familiar with relationships in which everything is negotiable; no one on either side of those relationships wants to work that way.

It is in areas of uncertainty that trust matters most. The work of healthcare is uncertain, because patients and their medical needs are variable. What needs to be done on any given day for any given patient is uncertain. In this setting, it is valuable to have cultural dynamics where people say "yes" without knowing the details, because the details are unknowable. Burt wrote, "You trust someone when you commit to a relationship before you know how the other person will behave. The more unspecified, take-for-granted, the terms of a relationship, the more trust is involved" (2005, p. 162).

Burt was describing what Putnam calls *thick trust*. No one can expect trust to emerge just at the moments when it is needed most; it is best built over time. Putnam wrote, "Frequent interaction among a diverse set of people tends to produce a norm of generalized reciprocity" (2020, p. 21). The denser the ties among people, the stronger the opportunities to build trust – and the ties among people working directly together in hands-on healthcare are about as dense as they come. In close-knit groups where bonding connections are strong, the manager can quickly detect and intervene when individuals are not responding to their colleagues or deviating from the group's norms.

Thick trust bound my internship group together. We were an ethnically and culturally diverse bunch and one of the first in which women comprised more than a third of the interns. We formed such strong bonds that I – and several of my fellow residents – married another group member. We have remained friends throughout the years even though our career trajectories have scattered us across the world.

Our mentors also contributed to our groups' cohesion. They knew who we were – not just our skill sets but what motivated us as people – so they knew how to get us to do our best in any situation, from covering another shift to responding to a code. Later, they occasionally nudged us along our career paths. In recent years, we've regrouped a time or two to honor our mentors' contributions to medicine and celebrate their retirements.

In contrast with thick trust – what you experience among close colleagues over time – *thin trust* is the sense that you can count on people whom you might see rarely or never at all. Putnam pointed out that "thin trust is even more useful than thick trust, because it extends the radius of trust" (2020, p. 136).

For example, thin trust among many types of stakeholders helped Israel keep its case mortality rate extraordinarily low during the first part of the COVID-19 pandemic.

Healthcare providers lost no time in collaborating with insurance companies and government agencies to reduce risks of transmission and implement vaccination programs with unusual speed. It took only three weeks to vaccinate 90% of the population age 60 and older. As noted by Eyal Zimlichman, chief medical officer at Sheba Medical Center: "We're used to times of emergency" (Zimlichman and Lee, 2021).

# The Instruments of Social Capital

Just as stocks, bonds, and annuities are instruments of financial capital, connections, social networks, and teams are the instruments of social capital. They create value and facilitate the flow of resources and information.

## Connections

Burt uses the phrase *structural holes* to describe the spaces between groups of people. Connections transmit information across these holes. Both Burt and Putnam describe two key types of connections – bonding connections and bridging connections.

*Bonding connections* are characterized by thick trust. They occur within groups – for example, when a team on a patient care unit meets for a safety huddle or gathers socially outside of work. Such interactions have an *inward* focus and are important for a sense of solidarity and identity.

*Bridging connections* occur *across* groups – for example, when caregivers from different departments or different hospitals get together. When connections like this work well, they help people to look *outward* and learn from each other.

Both types of connections play critical roles in the creation of social capital and deserve focused attention from managers and leaders. You need bridging connections to learn, and you need bonding connections to put that learning to work. Putnam references sociologist Xavier de Souza Briggs's distinction between the two – bonding social capital is essential for "getting by" while bridging social capital is critical for "getting ahead" (2020, p. 23).

Putnam described how these two types of connections influence how people look at themselves and relate to others. He wrote: "Bridging social capital can generate broader identities and reciprocity, whereas bonding social capital bolsters our narrower selves. . . . Bonding social capital constitutes a kind of sociological superglue, whereas bridging social capital provides a sociological WD-40" (2020, p. 23).

Superglue and WD-40 are two tools that account for about 80% of my successful efforts fixing things around my home – and I suspect that the building of bonding and bridging connections may account for about 80% of my successful efforts in management. What makes these connections so critical is the importance of the bidirectional flow of information, both within and across groups, and what happens when that information reaches the other side of the connection.

Evidence for the power of combining bonding and bridging connections (and thick and thin trust) can be found in the creative research of Brian Uzzi, a sociologist at Northwestern University's Kellogg School of Management. Uzzi studied predictors of success – both financially and critically – in Broadway musicals and found that the probability of success rose with the number of prior collaborations among key players like actors, producers, directors, composers, and choreographers – but only up to a point. With extremely high numbers of prior collaborations, the probability of success declined. The analyses suggested that the ideal combination was a history of prior collaboration among several, but not all, of the key artists.

If everyone had worked together before, the result could be just a reproduction of their prior work. But with the injection of new ideas from outside the core group, the result could be superb. An example cited in the paper was *West Side Story*, which combined the skills of Broadway veterans Leonard Bernstein (the composer), Jerome Robbins (the choreographer), and Arthur Laurents (the playwright) with those of newcomer lyricist Stephen Sondheim. The result, records show, was tension, disagreement, and irritation among the creators – but also something new and magical (Uzzi and Spiro 2005). While Uzzi's research wasn't conducted in the context of healthcare, it has a message for leaders in healthcare organizations: They need to support both kinds of connections, bridging and bonding.

The response to the Boston Marathon bombing illustrated the value of both connections. Within the Brigham – and the city's other level-one trauma centers (Massachusetts General Hospital, Beth Israel Deaconess Hospital, Tufts Medical Center, and Boston Medical Center) – trauma response teams had formed bonding connections during months of emergency drills. They had also formed bridging connections with one another and with the city's Emergency Medical Services. These connections enabled triage teams at the bombing site and ambulances carrying the injured to coordinate the transport to each of the centers so that none was overtaxed. As a result, there were no deaths among the scores of badly injured people treated at any of the hospitals.

## Social Networks

How do you go about strengthening and extending the connections that enable social capital? Key insights on that work can be found in *Connected: How Your Friends' Friends' Friends Affect Everything You Feel, Think, and Do* by Nicholas A. Christakis and James H. Fowler, which describes basic steps in building social networks and governing what values are transmitted across them. Their advice is heavily grounded in their research; it's also fun and even moving to read.

Christakis and Fowler describe two fundamental aspects of social networks. The first is "connection" – who is linked to whom. The second is contagion, which pertains to the values that flow across those connections. As Christakis and Fowler point out, social networks can transmit negative values, like racism, or they can transmit positive values, like charitable giving. It's not enough to build social capital by building and strengthening connections; we subsequently must use the social capital and transmit the right values across them (2009, p. 16).

The brilliant paper in which Christakis and Fowler brought these ideas to life was published in 2007 in the *New England Journal of Medicine.* In their 2009 book *Connected,* they present the work cited in that paper:

> [R]igorous epidemiological methods [were used] to show that if a friend of a friend of yours gains weight, you are more likely to gain weight—even if you don't know that friend of a friend. In fact, there was danger of weight gain even if the person gaining weight was a friend of a friend of a friend. The reason for the spread of obesity in this pattern is that norms are developing around us all the time, even if we are oblivious to them. If others are eating dessert, we are more likely to eat dessert. If others eat a healthier meal, we are more likely to do the same (p. 17).

Christakis and Fowler go on to explore the ways in which the *shape* of social networks matters. The first critical question is how many people we are connected to. But a second question is how interconnected the people with whom we have relationships are. For example, if you have five close friends, that is lovely. But if your five friends also know each other well, and *real* relationships exist among them, then the norms that exist spread more easily among them and are much more powerful.

The term that social network experts use for the interconnectedness among your connections is *transitivity.*

*A Primer on Social Capital*

Simply put, if your friends are tightly connected to each other, then you are all stuck together. You can't break off relationships with someone if you get in a spat, because you are going to be running into each other at book club or pot-luck supper night or some other social event. The connections among you are stronger because of the structure of your social network.

On a larger scale, social networks are more than the clusters around any one individual. Because people are influenced by those around them, large groups can move in one direction or another like a flock of birds or a school of fish. Christakis and Fowler provided convincing evidence that social networks have a life of their own: They are more like a single organism than a collection of organisms – an insight with powerful implications for leaders and managers.

## Teams

Within groups inside an organization, Burt described how the social capital of individuals aggregates to the social capital of their teams. He wrote: "Teams composed of people whose networks extend beyond the team to span structural holes in the company are significantly more likely to be recognized as successful" (2005, p. 45). In other words, a team where members talk only to each other is not as likely to be as effective as a team where members have meaningful contact with outsiders. Even worse is a team where members do not interact much or well with each other. The role of managers is to build reciprocity and trust – and thus connections – in their part of the organization, both among individuals and across groups.

Great teams are important assets for healthcare organizations. But the challenges of healthcare are constant, variable, and unpredictable. When problems arise, there often isn't the chance to build up thick trust, which may take years of working together, within teams. Harvard Business School professor Amy Edmondson suggests that forming teams should be a natural part of working together. She writes: "Teaming, coined deliberately to capture the *activity* of working together, presents a new, more flexible way for organizations to carry out interdependent tasks. Unlike the traditional concept of a team, *teaming* is an active process, not a static entity" (2012, p. 28).

She continues:

> It involves coordinating and collaborating without the benefit of stable team structures, because many operations, such as hospitals, power plants, and military installations, require a level of staffing flexibility that makes stable team composition rare. In a growing number of organizations, the constantly shifting nature of work means that many teams disband almost as soon as they've formed (p. 28).

In her book *Teaming*, Edmondson emphasizes the importance of learning. After all, new teams are usually pulled together because the traditional organizational structure is not ideal for new challenges. Edmondson believes that collective learning requires individuals to:

- Ask questions.
- Share information.
- Seek help.
- Experiment with unproven actions.
- Talk about mistakes.
- Seek feedback.

Edmondson recognized the barriers to these behaviors, and she has shown how the presence or absence of "psychological safety" helps explain why some teams are effective and others are not. Military teams, for example, have "after-action reviews" in which everyone understands that it is everyone's duty to speak up about mistakes that may have occurred. After all, repeating the mistake might cost lives. The same is true in healthcare, of course.

Edmondson's framework for successful teamwork requires "four behaviors: speaking up, collaboration, experimentation, and reflection. . . . These behaviors are enacted in iterative cycles. Each new cycle is informed by the results of the previous cycle. Cycles continue until desired outcomes are achieved" (2012, p. 105). In sum, teaming requires data to understand the challenge and assess progress; a culture within the group where there is a commitment to learn and improve; and the psychological safety needed for team members to throw out ideas, admit they were wrong, and prepare to try someone else's idea.

Like Edmondson, General Stanley McChrystal and colleagues realized that truly excellent teams – those in which the team members would do anything and everything for each other – were more flexible and thus more effective than troops organized in traditional ways. The military had a long history of creating superb teams like the celebrated Navy SEAL teams. But McChrystal recognized that the culture that brought strength to these teams was also a barrier to their cooperation.

The issue was the shared sense among members of teams that it was us against the world – including other members of the U.S. military! This sense was the superglue of bonding connections on steroids. As McChrystal put it:

> Imagine the closest roommate relationships you've ever had and multiply that by one hundred. The bonds within squads are fundamentally different from those between squads or other units. In the words of one of our SEALs, "The squad is the point at which everyone else sucks. That other squadron sucks, the other SEAL teams suck, and our Army counterparts definitely suck." Of course, every other squad thought the same thing (2015, p. 127).

These teams had fantastic bonding connections, but at the price of limited bridging connections. They had plenty of thick trust but little thin trust. McChrystal understood that he needed more than a large number of excellent teams to control Al Qaeda throughout the world; he needed those teams to work together, like a team of teams. He needed his teams throughout the world to learn from each other. He needed thin trust as well as thick trust. And he needed information to flow quickly throughout the network and be trusted and used immediately.

To describe the military application of social capital, McChrystal and his colleagues coined the phrase "team of teams." They did not want to lose the magic of the tight teams where every individual knew every other individual, where they all knew they shared a common purpose, where they had learned to trust each other over time and in so many varied circumstances.

These military teams have the same sense of reciprocity as my resident defined for me when he said, "We never say no to another intern here." McChrystal understood that it was possible to achieve that confidence in a group of 10 or 25 soldiers but impossible across a task force of 7,000. A different kind of functionality was needed to make those teams work together like a team of teams.

One important step that McChrystal took was to have conference calls every day at 8 a.m. in which representatives of every team throughout the world would share information related to Al Qaeda's activities and the effectiveness of their responses. For the next 22 hours, those teams would function with complete or near-complete autonomy, but all the while, their leaders knew that they would be convening again the next day as a team of teams.

This approach has been adopted and adapted in many healthcare organizations over the last decade. For example,

Intermountain Healthcare developed a tiered system of huddles with clear criteria for escalating issues, so that the critical issues reach executive leadership every day before 10:30 a.m. The six tiers and the times at which they meet throughout the system are:

1. 8:45 – Managers
2. 9:00 – Directors
3. 9:15 – Hospitals
4. 9:30 – Trauma/Community/Rural
5. 9:45 – Community Care/Specialty Care
6. 10:00 – Executive Leadership Team

The huddles are brief meetings in which participants stand around whiteboards. Leaders then write action plans, and follow-up is described in subsequent huddles (Harrison 2018). The subtext of the process to every manager was "You are the leader of a team . . . and that team is part of a team of teams."

Another version of huddling culture has been implemented at Meritus Health, where "instead of weekly 3-hour sit-down senior management meetings, the organization's dozen senior leaders adopted a system of daily 15-minute huddles in the hallway." They do daily improvement rounds in which leaders go to different parts of the organization to check in on how improvement initiatives are progressing. A visit to Meritus inspired the observation that leaders there need good shoes, because they don't spend much time in their offices alone looking at computers. The leaders of that system believe that more frequent action-oriented interactions have increased their speed in decision making and their sense of accountability (Joshi, 2022).

One of the most ambitious applications of the team-of-teams approach can be found in the "Command Center" of Jewish General Hospital, which is more than a hospital – it is a regional health network that has the Montreal Hospital as its hub. During the COVID pandemic, Jewish General Hospital was overwhelmed with patients, as were so many other institutions throughout the world. Among its responses was developing a Hospital-at-Home program, a program planned and implemented over a three-day weekend.

But another response (directly influenced by Team of Teams) has been to create a Command Center with data feeds that monitor the flow – or lack of flow – of patients throughout the network. The technology and its displays (including a large room in the basement of Jewish General with flat-screen monitors covering the walls) are impressive. But more impressive is the "human-ware" – the 8–10 huddles of leaders that occur throughout the day. Leaders from key departments – ranging from the emergency department to the ICUs to the Hospital-at-Home program, to patient transport, to housekeeping – come together to see where patients may be "stuck" and ready to move on, and they solve the problems together.

What can we learn from the five books mentioned at the top of this chapter? That social capital is based in reciprocity and trust, built by bonding and bridging connections among people, compounded through teamwork, and amplified across networks.

Building social capital requires forming both bonding and bridging connections and then using those connections to help the organization perform better. I make the case in the next chapter that this work is needed in healthcare now more than at any time in the past.

# Chapter 2

# Why Healthcare Needs Social Capital Now

Social capital has always been important in healthcare, but recent changes have made it more critical than ever. Ample evidence suggests that higher levels of social capital are associated with improved coordination of care, improved employee experiences, and faster adoption of evidence-based medicine. Increased social capital has also been associated with better clinical outcomes for patients, perhaps because better communication leads to shorter hospital stays and increased functional health.

The need for these positive effects of social capital has never been greater. Medical progress is helping people live longer and healthier lives, but its side effects complicate the work of everyone in healthcare. There are increasing constraints on financial and human capital. Healthcare costs are high and getting higher. More people are needed to deliver care for common conditions. Patients are making more visits to more clinicians, and coordination among those clinicians is far from perfect. Meanwhile, consumers' expectations are rising; they have grown accustomed to getting their needs met reliably and around the clock.

These side effects of progress can alarm patients and demoralize healthcare providers. At the same time, no one wants to slow the tide of progress. For managers and leaders, the path forward requires breaking the problems down into major categories and organizing to mitigate their impact.

This chapter describes changes that are occurring in medicine itself, in patients, in healthcare providers, and in society – laying the groundwork for considering what types of social capital will enable patients and caregivers to enjoy the benefits of modern medicine without the chaos.

## Medicine Is Changing

First, let's acknowledge that medical science and healthcare delivery have steeper hills to climb every year. The medical challenges that must be met constantly grow greater. People are living longer, which means that more people are needed to care for people with chronic conditions like diabetes and arthritis and degenerative conditions like Alzheimer's and Parkinson's disease. New pandemics are sweeping the globe every two to three years. There are epidemics of mental health issues, including substance abuse disorders, depression, anxiety, and loneliness.

To counter these problems, scientific advances have been nothing less than dazzling. To wit:

- New drugs, such as the glucagon-like peptide 1 (GLP-1) agonists for obesity and a range of other conditions

- New procedures using new devices, such as transcatheter aortic valve replacement (TAVR), which enables many patients with a narrowed aortic valve to be treated without having an open-heart procedure
- New tests, such as genetic markers that identify cancers that are likely to respond to targeted therapies that might slow growth with less toxicity

These are just a few examples, and there are so many more on the way.

## Costs Keep Rising

When critics of healthcare say, "Costs keep rising without detectable changes in quality," they are ignoring changes in patients' needs and in what can be done to help them. Healthcare today is not your parents' healthcare or even last year's healthcare. Those of us who take care of patients would never want to wind back the clock.

Nevertheless, the critics raise important concerns. Significant advances come with costs that have made healthcare affordability a crushing issue. That issue isn't top of mind for the scientists who are responsible for the breakthroughs and for the physicians who use them. Those scientists and physicians understandably think, "That is someone else's problem to solve. My concern is what might help patients."

Yet healthcare costs are a crushing problem for almost everyone now. They are an enormous problem for governments trying to hold taxes down, for employers trying to remain competitive, and for people struggling to manage their household budgets. High healthcare costs compromise the competitiveness of national economies. For example, if a technology company in the United States can hire a software engineer in another country at a salary that is lower than just the cost of family health insurance coverage for a comparably trained engineer in the United States, what is it going to do?

We like to hope that the costs associated with scientific advances will be offset by savings due to better health across society. I so wish that were true. The painful reality is that, in general, more care virtually always means higher net spending. And when healthcare spending increases, fewer funds are available for addressing social needs such as housing, education, and nutrition.

Healthcare was once a cost-plus culture in which health-care providers figured out what it cost to do what they did and then added a small margin. Then they negotiated for that amount, and the government and insurance companies eventually came around and got close to it. That cost-plus approach worked when government, insurers, and employers had the flexibility to increase spending on healthcare. However, that flexibility no longer exists because healthcare costs are so high and other needs have become more pressing.

Furthermore, more sophisticated care typically requires more people to deliver it, and these people frequently have narrow fields of expertise. They tend to have a laserlike focus on their specific issues. The result is that state-of-the-science care is not only more costly but also at risk for being less coordinated and more chaotic.

## Data Flow Is Becoming Overwhelming

Another product of medical progress is the flood of information being generated and used in the course of care. More tests mean more results. New treatments require more testing to assess impact and detect side effects. More clinicians involved means more notes being generated, and those notes are getting longer and longer.

The good news is that electronic medical records are getting better at pulling that information together. During the COVID pandemic, for example, physicians were quietly pleased to find that vaccination information from retail pharmacies started showing up in electronic medical records. More recently, I've been finding that notes from caregivers all over the country, like the Florida orthopedist who injected the knee of one of my patients, are appearing among the progress notes in my organization's electronic medical record – not all of the time, but a lot of the time. I don't have to go searching for them, electronically or otherwise.

The bad news is that the flow is overwhelming. I was trained to believe that I should read every word of every note and look at every lab result. That wasn't so difficult when care was simpler, patients saw fewer doctors, and fewer tests were done. Today, every patient has become a big data problem; electronic records get blamed because they bring all that information together. The notes themselves are cut-and-paste compilations that have all the information in them, but they are simply not digestible. The case study that follows details how New York University uses ChatGPT to tackle this problem.

---

### Case Study 2.1  NYU Langone Health: Using ChatGPT to Improve Communication

Social capital is not just how people interact with each other; it is also how they interact with their infrastructure. In the case of language models like ChatGPT, that infrastructure can improve care by helping humans communicate more clearly and effectively with each other.

NYU Langone Health recently described how it has used ChatGPT-4 to address one of the most annoying problems for clinicians – the deteriorating usefulness of progress notes in the electronic health record, or EHR (Feldman et al. 2024). Utility has steadily eroded due to the "every patient is a big data problem" phenomenon; clinicians are cutting and pasting long sections from prior notes into the notes from their encounters. The result is that errors are reproduced over and over. Even worse, people do not have the time or patience to read the notes.

NYU Langone Health leaders were moved to action by EHR vendor data showing that their organization's notes were in the bottom quartile for note brevity, suggesting that their notes were "bloated" compared

---

to those of other U.S. organizations – and they were aware that U.S. notes are reportedly four times as long as those in other countries. As described in the article in *NEJM Catalyst* about their initiative, "The leadership team sought an improvement strategy that would align with the existing culture that uses enterprise-wide dashboards and cross-specialty metrics to support transparency and drive improvement across the institution" (Feldman et al. 2024). In other words, NYU Health wanted to use social capital rather than heavy-handed interventions.

Their first step was to create an enterprise-wide structure for note quality measurement in September 2020. A leadership committee developed a multidimensional framework for assessing the quality of notes based on "5Cs":

1. *Completeness.* Does this note contain the following elements: appropriate history, appropriate examination, appropriate plan?
2. *Conciseness.* Does this note collect only pertinent data/information?
3. *Contingency (Discharge) Planning.* Does this note contain specific contingency planning to help the team plan the next steps?
4. *Correctness.* Is this note internally correct and consistent?

*(continued)*

*(continued)*

5. *Clinical Assessment and Reasoning.* Does this note have a differential diagnosis? Does the note commit to a diagnosis and comment if the patient is the same, better, or worse?

NYU Health's team tested the ability of experts to reliably score notes on all five dimensions as Yes, No, or Partial. Meanwhile, NYU Health clinicians were informed of the initiative and the scoring framework.

The expert scoring went well, and the model made sense to clinicians, but there was no way to have a human being review more than a handful of the notes generated by NYU Health clinicians. So the committee turned to their Information Technology department, which developed an AI model that could reliably grade large volumes of notes. Testing the model went well, and NYU Langone initiated note evaluation for its inpatient campuses. Patient-care unit leaders were trained to use an interactive dashboard that helped them follow the AI-generated note grades over time.

Lessons were learned. For example, AI models trained on internal medicine notes were found to perform poorly on notes written by clinicians in other specialties. Hyperlinks were built to help clinicians write better notes. Educational programs were created with a different "C" as the focus each month. The goal for each team was 15–20% relative improvement over the course of a year.

The results were startling. Figure 2.1 shows the percentage of clinical notes that the AI tool determined met the standards for note quality for each of the 5Cs over time. The education process was initiated in early 2021, and by the end of that year, compliance was above 90%, where it has stayed since. Note that the figure is a screen shot from the reporting tool that enabled users

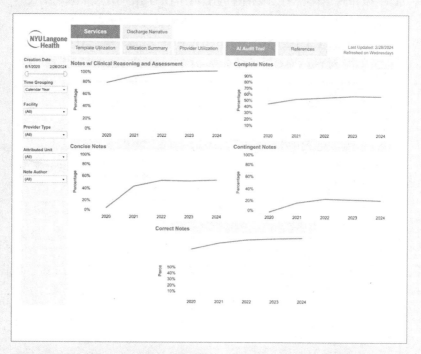

**Figure 2.1** Audit of compliance with standards of note quality.

*Source*: Artificial Intelligence (AI) Audit Tool on the NYU Langone Note Quality Dashboard (Feldman et al. 2024).

*(continued)*

*(continued)*

to choose a time frame and time grouping and to drill down to specific facilities, provider types, units, and even the notes' authors.

Figure 2.2 shows the increase in the percentage of notes meeting criteria for Clinical Assessment and Reasoning by month, along with information on the intervention stage. Note the major leaps that occurred with education (spreading information about the norm through NYU's social networks) and standardization (closure implemented through bonding connections).

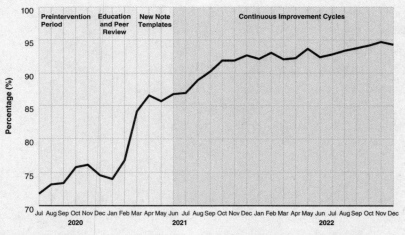

Note: The number of clinical notes assessed per month ranged from 15,338 in July 2020 to 21,448 in December 2022.

**Figure 2.2** Percentage of notes meeting criteria for clinical assessment and reasoning.
*Source*: Feldman et al. 2024. Reprinted with permission of *NEJM Catalyst* (http://catalyst.nejm.org); © Massachusetts Medical Society.

This case study provides an example of the creation of social capital both in the way clinicians at NYU worked together – adopting standards and working across disciplines – and with their infrastructure – embracing the use of AI/ChatGPT to augment a learning culture. It is a dazzling example of building social capital through both human connections and human–IT interactions to take on an important and complex challenge.

## Collaboration Across Organizations Is Growing

In the past, healthcare organizations tended to focus their information technology on connecting people under their own umbrellas. They wanted to do everything that patients needed by themselves.

But during the pandemic, that was simply not feasible. Retail pharmacies were better sites for vaccinations than doctors' offices in so many ways, particularly because they were more convenient for patients. The idea that convenience for patients is important became more compelling as patients got used to interacting with the world through the internet. The response of many healthcare organizations – albeit still far from complete – has been to enable patients to get laboratory testing, urgent care, and other care in locations that are more convenient, even though they are operated by other providers.

# Patients Are Changing

The Baby Boomers are aging, and, just as this generation has transformed education and marriage and every other institution that they have passed through, they are having an impact on healthcare. Moreover, the aging of the population will not slow down as Baby Boomers start to pass from the stage. Census projections are that the percentage of Americans 65 years of age and older will rise from 17% to 23% by 2050 (U.S. Census Bureau, 2023).

Data show that seniors today are better educated than in the past; the percentage with four years of college or more has increased from 5% in 1965 to 33% in 2023. They are working longer, and their poverty rates are lower. They are living in the community longer; the percentage living in nursing homes or other assisted living settings has declined (Mather and Scommegna 2024).

The bad news is that Americans of all ages are all too often socially isolated, and that epidemic of loneliness has important effects on their health. The Surgeon General's Report in 2023 estimates that lacking social connections can increase the risk for premature death as much as smoking 15 cigarettes per day does (Murthy 2023). That report captures a wide array of adverse health, economic, and societal effects that are associated with loneliness.

What is important to these aging, lonely Baby Boomers when it comes to their healthcare? Data from Press Ganey surveys show that their concerns have intensified over time. As has been true in the past, in every setting of care, Boomers are typical of patients of all ages. They place a high value on:

- *Teamwork*. They want their care to be well-coordinated.

- *Empathy.* They want their caregivers to genuinely care about them and to be responsive to their questions and worries.

- *Respect.* They want to be treated with courtesy, and they want their concerns to be considered credible.

## Patients' Confidence in Healthcare Is Increasing

Healthcare providers have been working hard to meet patients' needs, both clinical and emotional. As noted already, the challenges of doing so are always increasing, but providers have made real progress, and data show that patients appreciate it. For example, the percentage of patients giving a top "likelihood to recommend" to their hospitals started going up by about 1% per year beginning in 2008 (Lee 2016, p. 92). While patients' overall confidence in care at hospitals and emergency departments declined during the early years of the pandemic, it is now recovering. Remarkably, Press Ganey data show that patients' likelihood to recommend their office-based care continued to rise throughout the pandemic years. In short, things have been getting better; it just doesn't feel that way.

## Patients' Fears Are Intensifying

Despite their appreciation of the efforts of their providers, patients' fears have intensified in recent years. Patients are afraid of infections. They are afraid of errors that might injure them. They are afraid that opportunities to help them might be missed with all the activity swirling around them. Even when they *are* safe, they don't *feel* safe.

For example, patients' concern that their clinicians are not working together has increased. In 2023, for the first time, *teamwork* emerged in Press Ganey data as the top driver of "likelihood to recommend" in every care setting – hospitals, emergency departments, medical practices, and others. The consistency of this finding was startling for my colleagues in data analysis. Patients clearly know that there are more people involved in their care and that coordination among caregivers is far from perfect. That fact scares them.

Contributing to patients' fear is a sense that they are not respected. Patients are afraid their concerns are not being heard or believed or taken seriously. Since the murder of George Floyd on May 25, 2020, equity and inclusion have emerged as issues for almost everyone – not just groups defined by race, ethnicity, and gender. The care of people who are overweight and people with intellectual and physical disabilities has long produced cringeworthy moments, and it still does today. Now, however, there is a growing sense that everyone's dignity is challenged.

Patients' fears about safety are apparent in all their healthcare interactions, not just when they are in the hospital. This is a change from the early years of this century, when, for good reason, the safety movement focused on hospital care. The hospital was where quality measurement and improvement infrastructures were, and where patients were often frail and undergoing aggressive interventions. However, most people are not in hospitals, and, these days, *everyone* is worried about their risk of being harmed – and not without cause.

Recent research shows that errors remain common both for hospitalized patients (Bates et al. 2023, pp. 142–153) and for patients receiving outpatient care (Levine et al. 2024, pp. 238–748). Adverse drug events were the most frequent outpatient errors revealed in this research, followed by healthcare-associated infections and surgical or procedural events. Across multiple study sites, 1.8% to 23.6% of patients experienced at least one adverse event; rates were higher among older adults.

Although government-sponsored surveys (Consumer Assessment of Healthcare Providers & Systems, or CAHPS) still do not include questions about safety, my colleagues at Press Ganey have added four optional questions about safety concerns to our medical practice surveys and quickly were able to amass information from tens of millions of patients. We found that about 16% of patients *did* have safety concerns during their office visits, and those patients were unlikely to recommend their care providers – even if they rated the physician perfect for every physician-related function.

The bottom line: Patients are less trusting than in the past. They are unnerved when they see medical staff wear scrubs with stains from blood or other body fluids. They may see litter or something like a bandage with a spot of blood lying on the floor, and even though they know that the bandage is not likely to hurt them, they think, "Yuck," and are likely to wonder what else might go wrong.

## Patients Are Behaving More Like Customers

The rise of consumerism accelerated during the pandemic, when so many people became much more comfortable using the internet. A decade ago, I often heard physician colleagues arguing (I do mean arguing!) about the distinctions between patients and customers. But, at this point in healthcare history, the difference among these groups is blurring; the needs of patients and the demands of customers increasingly overlap.

That should come as no surprise – after all, customers and patients *are* the same human beings, and always have been. Today, however, they shift from one mode to the other instantly, and the internet provides them with ready access to information as well as a vehicle to express their feelings, both negative and positive.

Survey data from Press Ganey in 2023 showed that online search tools have surpassed doctor referrals as the most important influences for patients choosing a physician. Respondents indicated that they were 3.1 times more likely to rely on digital sources like directories, social media, and online search tools than on provider referrals when choosing a new primary care physician (PCP). They did their homework – reading an average of five reviews and visiting two or three sites before choosing a provider.

These data may be influenced by the fact that respondents were surveyed electronically, so they were likely comfortable with web-based tools. Still, the trends toward consumerism and away from the "Ask Your Doctor" mentality are striking. The proportion of respondents who said that they relied on provider referrals declined 21.3% in one year, and reliance on word-of-mouth referrals from acquaintances fell 43.5%.

Most of the respondents (83.5%) said that they go online at least occasionally to read reviews about a provider to whom they have been referred. Nearly half said they always or frequently did. And 30% said that they would be discouraged from choosing a provider who had no reviews online.

From my own primary care practice, I can tell you that many of my patients now assume that I am not going to make them come into Boston and park near my hospital for an in-person visit unless they need to be examined or want an in-person interaction. I am perfectly fine with doing a virtual visit, and we are both happier because I do not have to apologize for the hassle of coming into town. I also tend to run on time because patients are not tied up in traffic.

Patients also now expect to communicate with my practice and me 24/7. The volume of patients' messages to their physicians increased about 150% almost overnight when COVID hit, and data show that the increase was even greater for women physicians than for their male counterparts (Kelleher 2024). Expectations for getting needs met smoothly and quickly are particularly high among younger patients, who consistently give lower overall likelihood-to-recommend ratings to their providers. These demographic differences suggest that loyalty to organizations will be harder to win in the years ahead.

For physicians and other clinicians, the in-basket monster is never far from one's thoughts. It is a constant worry, one that wears them down. Clinicians know that while they are trying to focus all their attention on one patient's needs, two other patients are sending them messages. Those messages have questions or requests for information that are important to the patients who sent them; those patients are delighted when the responses come right away and disappointed when they do not. The same stream of new messages is flowing in when clinicians are driving to and from work, chatting with a friend or family member, or sleeping.

For clinicians (especially doctors), the result is a constant sense that one is falling behind. That's not fun for people who are hard-wired to be conscientious. There is an urge to cut short other activities and get back to the inbox. Their families sense their inability to be "in the moment" during off-work hours and complain about it.

Clinicians know that it is not a bad thing that patients feel "connected" and that they can reach out to their caregivers at any time. But the in-basket feels like a monster and is widely recognized as a major contributor to burnout.

Many organizations have transitioned from talking about the in-basket monster to doing something about it – or, more accurately, decreasing the burden on the physicians who are the targets of so many of the messages. Heavy-handed measures like charging patients for interactions via patient portal messages have not had much traction; clinicians don't like having one more thing to keep track of, such as the time it took them to respond, and they worry about not treating all patients the same. But multidimensional social capital interventions have led to impressive results in some delivery systems.

Case Study 2.2 illustrates how Atrius Health employed teamwork to tackle its burgeoning in-basket problem.

---

### Case Study 2.2  Atrius Health: Using Social Capital to Take on the In-Basket Monster

Atrius Health, a large multispecialty group with about 30 locations in the Boston area, decided to take on the in-basket challenge in 2017. Atrius has a long tradition of team care, reflecting its roots in managed care. It was started in 1969 as Harvard Community Health Plan (HCHP), one of the first staff-model health maintenance organizations in the eastern United States. Over the years, HCHP grew, added new providers, and changed its name multiple times, but it always remained a multidisciplinary physician group with a full array of other staff to care for several hundred thousand patients. Atrius Health was (and remains) independent of hospitals but has had close partnerships with hospitals. That said, the organization's cultural DNA is to use teamwork to keep people healthy and out of the hospital.

Despite that teamwork orientation, Atrius's physicians have not been immune to the epidemic of burnout. Atrius's leaders quickly recognized the importance of the in-basket monster and saw that in-basket processes

*(continued)*

---

*(continued)*

simply did not resonate with a team-based model. They needed a social solution, not one based on modifying the work of individual physicians. They started a long-term multidimensional initiative in 2017 and described their extraordinary progress over the next five years in a 2023 article by Jane F. Fogg and Christine A. Sinsky in *NEJM Catalyst*.

Atrius's progress did not occur overnight, and no single tactic served as a magic bullet. It began with leadership commitment to the goal of reining in the in-basket monster and aligning managers around a planned five-step approach:

1. Examine the current state.
2. Develop a strategic approach.
3. Create governance and work groups.
4. Establish and execute tactics for each in-basket message type.
5. Measure the impact of each intervention.

The first step, examine the current state, required detailed data analysis of the different types of communications flowing to different types of clinicians. As they plunged into these data, they recognized their complexity but did not get overwhelmed. As they wrote in their article: "There were no simple or singular tactics that could address all message types or folder types. Our strategy required a multipronged approach. We would work on multiple folders where opportunities were found and look to the sum total of many smaller interventions. . . . We considered patient experience, safety, and quality outcomes with each intervention" (Fogg and Sinsky 2023).

As they developed their approaches to the different message types, they found that they were asking a series of questions in each context:

- Could we simply remove some messages entirely as opposed to delegating them to another team member?

- Could we employ automation for routine tasks, removing all team members from the task?

- Could we advance delegation with protocols and systems design that routed the message directly to the team member, bypassing the PCP?

They settled on four basic tactics:

1. *Elimination.* Complete removal of the waste and duplication from the in-basket

2. *Automation.* Employing protocols and direct routing to task completion, like routing normal laboratory results directly to the patient without sending them to the physician's inbox

3. *Delegation.* Routing the task to a team member to resolve independently

*(continued)*

*(continued)*

**4.** *Collaboration.* Sharing responsibility for message types across team members or coverage departments

The details of how they implemented these tactics can be found in Fogg and Sinsky (2023).

Table 2.1 shows the reduction in the volume of in-basket messages achieved from 2017 to 2022 in various categories as well as the major tactic used. Over this period, the daily in-basket volume was reduced from 61.6 per day to 42 for a typical PCP (which included physicians and advanced practice providers, such as physician assistants and nurse practitioners) – a 32% reduction.

**Table 2.1** Atrius in-basket volume reduction, 2017–2022.

| In-basket category | Baseline in-basket volume per day per full-time PCP (2017) | Volume reduction achieved (2022) | Tactic used |
| --- | --- | --- | --- |
| Media manager | 5 | 98% | Eliminate |
| CC charts | 13 | 35% | Eliminate |
| ED/hospital ADT messages | 3 | 100% | Eliminate |

| In-basket category | Baseline in-basket volume per day per full-time PCP (2017) | Volume reduction achieved (2022) | Tactic used |
|---|---|---|---|
| Prescription renewals | 16 | 50% | Automate |
| Laboratory test results | 19 | 30% | Automate (normal results); delegate (abnormal results) |
| Patient medical advice request | 5 | 40% | Collaborate |

PCP, primary care physicians; CC, carbon copy, or communications/notes on which the PCP is copied; ED, Emergency Department; ADT, "Ask the Doctor" messages from patients.

*Source*: Adapted from Table 1, Fogg and Sinsky 2023.

Both "bridging connections" and "bonding connections" were critical to Atrius's success. Working across disciplines was essential. As the authors described:

> We discovered more possibilities combining IT and clinical operations design and uniting clinical needs with EHR design feasibility. For example, our clinical

leaders did not know how our in-basket systems were designed, such as why a document was routed to them. Our IT leaders did not know what the PCP needed to manage patient care needs, such as which team member could best address the document. Working together, we learned that the design of information flow was sometimes very intentional and sometimes not. Many dispensations were simply "route to PCP" when the intention and purpose of the message were ill defined. We discovered system design flaws stemming from our history of siloed leadership; the design of some routine protocols as individualized to each department and site, creating a complex web of routing protocols (Fogg and Sinsky 2023).

They needed communication across bridging connections, but they also needed buy-in across bonding connections. The very next sentences in their article were:

A degree of standardization across the organization was needed to implement systems' approaches to in-basket reduction—specifically, standardization of common clinical workflows, such as renewing medications, telephone triage, or physician-to-physician communication. Standardization of clinical practice has merits and challenges. . . . Our collaboration between clinical and IT leadership helped us understand the necessity of targeted standardization (Fogg and Sinsky 2023).

There is beauty in the detail of what they standardized and how they did it – albeit beauty that only people who have been immersed in patient care can appreciate.

They created a practice agreement with their specialists on what and what not to send to PCPs. For example, new consultations should be sent, as should notes for visits in which there were significant changes in prognosis or condition or when there were actions the PCP should take. All sent notes were to have an attached comment explaining why it was sent and the recommended actions.

Figure 2.3 shows the sustained reduction in "CC" notes to PCPs over time. The Y-axis shows the number of unique in-basket messages per clinical full-time equivalent PCP. Atrius saw rapid improvement when it implemented the intervention in 2017 Quarter 3. A second drop occurred when COVID-19 hit in the spring of 2020.

The steady decline over the years demonstrates the importance of group learning and the adoption of behavioral norms, which takes time. When I read this manuscript in my role as editor-in-chief after it was submitted to *NEJM Catalyst*, my first reaction was as a doctor. I thought, "I don't have time to learn how to standardize what I do so I can work in a system like this." Then I saw that the in-basket volume for PCPs was reduced by about 30%. And my next reaction was "I don't have time *not* to work in a system like this."

Few healthcare leaders think they can afford to ignore patient expectations, like 24/7 availability of their physicians. The risk of losing patients to competitors is greater than at any time in the past because loyalty to brands of all types has decreased (Villa 2023). Recognizing that not all patients

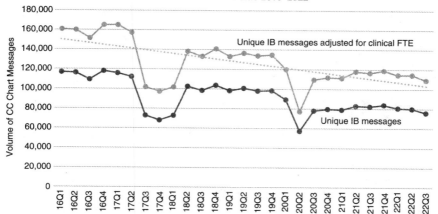

**Figure 2.3** Trends in volume of CC chart messages and CC chart volume, 2016–2022.
*Source*: Feldman et al. 2024. Reprinted with permission of *NEJM Catalyst* (http://catalyst.nejm.org); © Massachusetts Medical Society.

are alike, organizations are collecting data so that they can segment them into groups with similar tendencies. And these organizations are refreshing their data and analyses constantly – because the one thing that all these segments have in common is that they are not standing still.

# Healthcare Providers Are Changing

Doctors are changing, and so is doctoring. Physicians are far from the only people who matter among healthcare providers, but their issues are generalizable to others working in this sector.

Simply put, there are too few physicians today, too much work to do, and too much information that must be absorbed and used to provide optimal patient care. The average age of physicians in the United States is 53.9 years (Definitive Healthcare 2023), which is more than a decade older than the rest of the workforce. As physicians retire, they are being replaced by new physicians with different approaches to their lives and work.

Fewer than half of physicians (44% in 2022 compared with 53% in 2012) are now in private practice. Among physicians under age 45, only 32% own their own practices (Smith, 2023). More than half of medical school graduates are now women, and those who have children earn about $3.1 million less over the course of their career than their male counterparts (Skinner et al. 2023). The male–female gap in hours worked was 0.6% for single physicians but 17.5% for physicians with children. These data reflect what everyone knows – that women physicians with children are doing more at home than most of their male counterparts.

Many physicians – especially women – are deciding that the pressures are too great, and they just don't want to keep practicing medicine. With colleagues from Press Ganey, I coauthored a digital article in *Harvard Business Review* called "Why So Many Women Physicians Are Quitting" (Dudley et al. 2022). Women physicians spend more time talking to patients and corresponding with them afterward and do a more thorough job documenting their interactions. We described data demonstrating that women physicians were not only under greater pressure at work but also less able to recover from their clinical work once they were home:

A gender gap was particularly apparent when physicians were surveyed on their ability to decompress when they returned home from work. Female physicians had lower scores than male physicians on all four areas of decompression (numbers are on a scale of 1–5, with 5 being best), including enjoying personal time without worrying about work (females: 3.39; males: 3.61), freeing their mind from work while away (females: 3.22; males: 3.43), disconnecting from work communications (females: 3.20; males: 3.41), and rarely losing sleep over work issues (females: 3.31; males: 3.51). Because this gap persisted across all female physicians ages 30 through 65, the difference cannot be explained as time-limited challenges of child-rearing responsibilities (Dudley et al. 2022).

The cumulative impact of these trends is that every time a physician retires more than one physician is required to replace the retiree. That is because the replacements do not see as many patients as the retiring doctors did. It is not that the new doctors are lazy; the real problem is that modern medicine is burning them out.

The driver of that burnout is partly "too much work," but it is also "too much to know." "Too much" in this context is the volume of information flowing toward physicians. "Too much" does not mean "more than I want" – it really does mean *too much*. I coauthored an article in the *New England Journal of Medicine* with Ziad Obermeyer, an emergency medicine physician and machine-learning expert, that described the information overload problem and considered the inevitable paths forward. We noted in the article that the amount of information available on individual patients has simply become too much for the human brain to handle:

> All this information strains our collective ability to think. Medical decision making has become maddeningly complex. Patients and clinicians want simple answers, but we know little about whom to refer for *BRCA* testing or whom to treat with PCSK9 inhibitors. Common processes that were once straightforward – ruling out pulmonary embolism or managing new atrial fibrillation – now require numerous decisions.
>
> So, it's not surprising that we get many of these decisions wrong. Most tests come back negative, yet misdiagnosis remains common. Patients seeking emergency care are often admitted to the hospital unnecessarily, yet many also die suddenly soon after being sent home. Overall, we provide far less benefit to our patients than we hope. These failures contribute to deep dissatisfaction and burnout among doctors and threaten the health care system's financial sustainability (Obermeyer and Lee 2017, p. 1210).

The implication is that the individual doctor simply cannot provide good care to many, if not most, patients. Instead, the correct unit of analysis should be the entire team, including nonphysicians, and the team should be augmented by the use of advanced information systems. There are still physicians who see themselves as solo practitioners, and there is much to be admired in the pride that many of them bring to their work. But physicians who cannot work well in teams and who do not learn to use artificial intelligence are being replaced by physicians who can.

The cultural shifts entailed in all these changes are daunting. Morale is low among physicians in most organizations and burnout is high. Physicians' professional lives are fragmented – for example, hospitalists now assume the care of inpatients at most hospitals – and there are no more doctors' dining rooms. Physicians might go through a whole day without talking to other physicians involved in the care of their patients, or to any other physicians at all.

Variations on these themes apply to other clinicians, especially nurses, nurse practitioners, and physician assistants. The sense that the status quo isn't working is reflected in burnout, in earlier-than-planned departures from the workforce, in difficulty hiring, and in retiring employees.

## Society Is Changing

The rise of consumerism has already been noted in the description of how patients are changing. On a societal scale, there are expectations of transparency on all issues, especially quality of care. In 2013, the University of Utah became the first major organization to post online all comments patients made after office visits with their physicians. Today, the number of institutions that do not do this is rapidly dwindling.

Another powerful trend is financial pressure, which is increasingly intense for every type of organization in healthcare. These pressures are only going to become more intense because costly new treatments like biologic medications and gene therapy are in the pipeline. Taxpayers are not going to vote for higher taxes, and employers competing in a global economy cannot afford annual increases in costs of 6 to 8%.

Since 1995, one physician friend had been telling me, "People are always saying that healthcare is about to undergo revolutionary change. And then I look up five years later, and things are basically the same."

He is not saying that anymore. "This time," he said to me recently, "I think it's real." And he agrees that working harder is not going to help healthcare providers address cost issues and pressures for better quality. He agrees that we have to take on the chaos that results from the complexity of modern medicine.

We talked about how, earlier in our careers, friends would occasionally tell us about how family members were admitted to our hospital and had a less-than-ideal experience. We used to say "Why didn't you call me?" Today, we ruefully agreed, we tend to just nod and stay silent, and think to ourselves "Thank God you didn't call me."

To solve these problems, we are going to need real teams and do real redesign of care. We are going to need to use AI in smart ways that reduce costs and errors – and we are all going to have to use it. We're going to need to figure out how to deal with depressing societal trends like diminishing trust and respect.

In short, we need social capital.

# Chapter 3

# Building, Strengthening, and Using Social Capital Connections

Connections are as important to social capital as markets are to financial capital, and in a way, the two are a lot alike. Financial markets grow and strengthen when conditions are favorable; so do connections – and both tend to do well when people are doing well. As a rule, market values rise when employment is high and interest rates are low. Connections increase when people feel safe, recognized, and respected. While I have compared the chief officer (CO) for social capital to the organization's chief financial officer (CFO), COs for social capital have an advantage – they can establish a growth environment, while CFOs can only hope for one.

A CO for social capital can build connections at any level of the healthcare system – patients, employees, teams, and the organization. Each level has its own climate and culture. The work ahead is to modify the climate and culture so that connections can thrive. In general, these connections need to:

- *Foster a culture of respect.* Ideally, every person should feel that they are treated with respect. That simple basic need is a requirement that must be met if people are to participate in building social capital.

- *Promote pride.* The work of healthcare is noble but difficult and will always be characterized by uncertainty and disappointments. Given the uncertainties regarding ultimate outcomes, patients *must* have confidence in the skills and the values of those caring for them, and they can gain that confidence from caregivers who are proud of the quality of their organizations' care. That pride cannot rely solely on prominent brands or past achievements; rather, it should reflect the combination of high standards and a growth mindset. Pride is not sustainable just by trying to stay excellent; it requires constant improvement efforts. For this reason, true pride is based on a combination of confidence and humility.

- *Create trust.* Patients/consumers as well as people delivering care must feel confident that they will be treated fairly in circumstances that they have not yet imagined. To be trusted in this way, one must be trustworthy. Frances Frei's model in which trust is built through three elements – empathy, authenticity, and logic – is helpful as one works to establish trustworthiness at each level (Frei and Morriss 2020).

- *Develop a high reliability culture.* The concept of high reliability as performance as intended consistently over time is one that is useful for all aspects of care delivery. The fundamental principles of high-reliability organizations are transparency, communication, respect for expertise, and continuous learning and improvement. Applying these principles builds connections; deviating from them erodes connections.

- *Ensure psychological safety.* The CO of social capital must make it known that employees are welcome to express ideas and make suggestions without fear of reprisal and with the understanding that all teammates are accountable for their actions. Managers can create a "safe place" by acknowledging criticism without rebuttal or anger and by adopting productive suggestions from their reports.

- *Use crises as opportunities to build connections.* In *Bowling Alone*, Putnam (2020) pointed out how crises in the first half of the 20th century – the Depression and World War II – strengthened social capital in American communities. In healthcare, crises should be seen as opportunities to do the same. For patients, illness is a crisis; but it is also an opportunity for caregivers to earn and build trust. For organizations, externalities such as pandemics or economic pressures can threaten their business viability. These crises should also be recognized as opportunities to use social capital and build more.

## Connections with Patients

This chapter puts patients first for the same reason that the Mayo Clinic says its primary value is "The Needs of the Patient Come First" and the Cleveland Clinic says its "guiding principle" is "Patients First." Patients are the focus of healthcare – but patients don't always feel that is true. They can easily feel overlooked or even forgotten, confused about what is happening and what happens next. Their family members share their anxieties.

*Building, Strengthening, and Using Social Capital Connections*

Care cannot be considered successful unless patients and their families trust their caregivers. The simple phrase taught to me by a colleague, Cynthia Bero, long ago was that patients want "peace of mind that things are as good as they could be given the cards that they have been dealt." It's a little wordy, but I haven't come up with anything better; whenever I quote it, people nod, because that's what they want, too. Even if care is technically superb and clinical outcomes *are* as good as they could possibly be, total care is not successful unless patients have that peace of mind.

## Building Connections with Patients

For every caregiver to connect with every one of their patients is an essential part of excellence in care delivery – and trust is essential in building that connection. So is respect.

"Respect" may seem amorphous, but at least one party recognizes when it is absent – the person who feels disrespected. Researchers like Mary Catherine Beach (2024) of Johns Hopkins are sharpening our understanding of the following themes that characterize respect:

- Recognizing the unconditional value (dignity) of each person
- Treating patients as equals
- Listening to patients and not dismissing their concerns
- Knowing patients as individuals
- Being polite
- Responding to suffering

Beach's work – including analyses of data with my colleagues at Press Ganey – has also characterized examples of disrespect:

- Being treated like trash
- Not being treated as a person
- Being treated rudely or ignored
- Not having concerns listened to or taken seriously
- Being stereotyped
- Being talked down to

Beach points out that healthcare has traditionally thought of respect for patients as synonymous with autonomy by getting their consent for interventions on their behalf. But respect today has a bigger meaning, one related to social justice. At the core is seeing every person as equally valuable.

Comments from patient surveys provide strong evidence for the "Anna Karenina principle." This principle refers to the first line from Tolstoy's novel about marriage and relationships in 19th-century Russia: "Happy families are all alike; every unhappy family is unhappy in its own way." As applied to healthcare, my colleagues and I have found that a small number of common themes characterize positive patient experiences – the healthcare equivalent of Tolstoy's happy families – while a wide variety of missteps can unsettle patients and compromise their trust in their care (Guney et al. 2021).

By far, the most powerful of the common positive themes were courtesy and respect. Nothing else came close. These data suggest that building connections with patients is simply not possible unless patients feel respected by their caregivers.

The connections between patients and their clinicians have an increasing number of variations, but one thing holds true: They can never be taken for granted. There are traditional doctor–patient relationships, such as between primary care physicians and their patients, but, increasingly, advanced practice providers, such as nurse practitioners and physician assistants, are assuming critical roles at the front lines of primary and specialty care. And new models of care delivery are making their way into the marketplace. For example, many insurance products provide a strong incentive for "virtual first" care, where, in non-emergency situations, patients log in to their online accounts and get a virtual consultation before any in-person appointment is scheduled.

The exact title of the caregiver whom patients turn to first is not really that important; nor is the choice between virtual and in-person care. What matters is that patients are confident they are connected, so when they need access or information, they know how to reach out and get help as quickly as they need it.

Connections matter not just to individual patients; families frequently want to be involved, too. Patient confidentiality issues can be tricky, and the default norm should be that individual patients are confident that they alone control the flow of information about their medical care. But, just as parents are deeply involved in decisions about the care of their children, families are deeply involved in the care of many patients at the other end of life. Family participation in the care of elderly patients has become increasingly important as the Baby Boomers reach their 80s and beyond.

When family members feel no connection and do not trust the care the patient is receiving, the dynamics are terrible for them, for the patient, and for the clinicians as well. Also problematic is when every family member wants to talk to the physician one at a time and then they do not agree with the care plan or each other, or when the family connects with one clinician – usually a doctor or a nurse – but does not feel connected to the larger team that may be involved in the patient's care.

Consequently, an important part of building connections for patients today is understanding that the relationship is often broader than simply doctor–patient – it is increasingly the relationship between the care team and the family. There is a reason that the staff in most intensive care units are well practiced in arranging meetings between families of critically ill patients and multiple members of the teams taking care of them. Clinicians who have been part of those meetings know this: You don't end the meeting until every family member has asked every question they want to ask and the family knows that the members of the team agree. In technical terms, "we have our act together."

The fact is that arranging such meetings can be cumbersome for both the family and the clinicians, especially since family members can be scattered around the world. Fortunately, one positive outcome of the COVID-19 pandemic

*Building, Strengthening, and Using Social Capital Connections*

was that so many people became comfortable with virtual-meeting technology.

Group meetings of clinicians and family are excellent examples of the social capital created by the flow of information over connections with transitivity among the participants. For example, my first Zoom family meeting was arranged by a nurse practitioner for an elderly patient hospitalized for both kidney and heart failure (Lee 2021). In the patient's room were the patient, the nurse practitioner (holding an iPad), and the patient's daughter. Everyone else was online – the patient's wife in their home outside Boston, their son in a nearby suburb, and the patient's brother in California. The clinicians included the palliative care attending physician, the inpatient nephrologist, the patient's longtime outpatient nephrologist, a cardiologist on the heart failure service, and me – the patient's primary care physician.

Following the instructions of the nurse practitioner, who suggested the meeting and arranged the scheduling, the clinicians met for 15 minutes before the family joined. We wanted to be sure we agreed about the key issues for the patient, the most important of which was what would it take for him to be safe at home. Our discussion took a bit longer than 15 minutes, and the nurse practitioner had to remind us that the family was waiting in the waiting room. (We were all struck by the fact it somehow felt worse to keep people waiting in virtual waiting rooms than in real-life waiting rooms.) However, when our family meeting ensued, the conversation was brisk and effective. Everyone agreed that while the meeting had not been easy to schedule, it provided peace of mind and probably saved time for all of us.

Connections with patients can be expanded even beyond the family and care team through patient and family advisory councils (PFACs) – groups of patients, family members, and healthcare professionals who meet regularly – that generally serve as sounding boards for proposals to modify patient care or launch new programs.

Two recent developments are enhancing the impact of PFACs. One is the recognition that organizations should consider having multiple PFACs rather than just one, because these councils have traditionally been dominated by mostly white, heterosexual, and community members without disabilities. At the University of Rochester Medical Center, for example, there are now PFACS for BIPOC (Black, indigenous, and other people of color) patients; LGBTQIA+ (people who identify as lesbian, gay, bisexual, transgender, queer or questioning their gender, intersex, asexual, or their allies) patients; deaf patients, and others (Beckerman 2024).

The other development is the ability of technologies like virtual focus groups and crowdsourcing to gain insights from groups of people, such as the participants in PFACs. Just getting these groups together, online or otherwise, can create new knowledge as members interact with each other and generate ideas for improvement. But recording the meetings and using artificial intelligence (AI) to capture and analyze verbal comments and even facial expressions and eye movements can markedly increase the yield of information.

## Strengthening Connections with Patients

Like muscles, connections grow stronger with use. This is especially true for hospitalized patients; the more often a clinician looks in on them, the safer they feel in that person's care.

Figure 3.1 shows the correlation between patients' overall likelihood of recommending hospitals in CAHPS surveys and how often patients recalled nurses rounding on them. The clear message from these data is that meaningful hourly rounding, where the nurses have a real interaction with their patients, is one of the most effective ways to give patients confidence that they are in good hands. The generalizable principle is that the more interactions patients have with their caregivers, the more confident they are in their care. And the sicker they are, the greater the impact

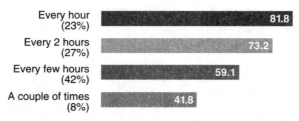

**Figure 3.1** Correlation between patients' "recommend the hospital" scores and nurse rounding frequency. X-axis = Percentage of respondents recommending hospital for each frequency of rounding; Y-axis = Percentages of nurses at each rounding frequency.
*Source*: Press Ganey, proprietary data.

on their confidence. As my colleague Chrissy Daniels puts it, "The secret is not doing new things. It is doing our best things more often."

Interacting frequently is particularly important in strengthening connections with nonphysicians and teams and in virtual interactions facilitated by telemedicine or online chats. Traditional healthcare is a low-frequency, high-stakes interaction; patients are often trusting because of their familiarity with the process. As new care models become common, it is important to build familiarity and trust through high-frequency, low-stakes interactions.

The portals associated with electronic health records provide low-stakes interactions. It is important to encourage caregivers to respond to requests made through portals promptly. Patients' trust that the system is taking care of them grows if they get prompt responses to their requests for appointments, prescriptions, and information. Moreover, the more they use their portal, the more comfortable they become with its functions and its interface. No one likes figuring out how a new app or web interface works; one that is familiar provides an additional reason to stay loyal to a provider.

While electronic communication can strengthen social capital during periods of calm in patients' medical lives, every illness should be recognized as a time of crisis for patients and an opportunity to strengthen connections in person. Following the basic principle of "the more contact, the better" is especially important. Not only do data clearly demonstrate the value of purposeful hourly rounding by nurses when patients are hospitalized; data also demonstrate that checking in on patients when they are at home builds their trust.

## Using Connections with Patients

Connections with patients should always be used to convey respect, pride, trust, teamwork, and high reliability. Every interaction is an opportunity to reinforce messages, including these:

- You are respected. We are interested in what you have to say. We believe you.
- You are why we are here.
- You can be confident that your care is in the hands of good people.
- You are in the hands of a good team; we are all working together.
- We are going to keep you safe. Our goal is Zero Harm to you.

Patients are ready to strengthen their connections with their providers through reciprocity (Lee et al. 2023). When comments from patient experience surveys were analyzed by AI, it became apparent that trust grows when patients perceive that caregivers trust their knowledge of their own bodies as well as when caregivers demonstrate caring behaviors. As one surveyed patient commented: "Dr. [X] . . . validated my knowledge of the disease and trusted that I know my body and how I respond to treatment."

In short, to earn patients' trust and respect, caregivers should demonstrate trust and respect for them.

## Connections with Individual Employees

Organizations cannot build social capital with patients unless they build social capital with their employees and with other workers who are deeply involved in delivering care. Return on investment (ROI) for social capital among individual caregivers is direct and immediate because it enhances employee retention. Press Ganey data strongly suggest that social capital with employees will also have an ROI based on improved safety, quality, and efficiency of care delivery.

Just as healthcare delivery should focus on every patient as an individual, managers must regard all the people reporting to them as individuals as well. And, as is true of patients, every employee should feel respected, valued, and included. Employees should trust that the organization will do all it can to keep them safe. They should be proud to be working where they work and doing what they do.

These goals are supported by Press Ganey data like the engagement survey responses from 410,000 healthcare employees. In these analyses, my colleagues identified risk factors for employees' readiness to look for another job by examining what factors were associated with a low level of agreement with the statement that they expected to be working for their organization in three years.

Employees were asked how strongly they agreed with a series of statements by responding using numbers 1 through 5, with 1 representing "I strongly disagree" and 5 representing "I strongly agree." For example, those who answered "1" to "I like the work I do" were 8.5 times more likely to answer "1" to "I plan to be working here in three years" than those who answered "5" to "I like the work I do."

The next list describes risk factors and their strength associated with employees' readiness to consider leaving:

- I like the work I do. (8.5)
- My work is meaningful. (7.0)
- The work I do makes a real difference. (6.5)
- I see every patient as an individual person with specific needs. (6.1)
- This organization provides high-quality care and service. (6.0)
- This organization conducts business in an ethical manner. (4.5)
- This organization treats employees with respect. (4.3)
- This organization values employees from different backgrounds. (4.3)
- My job makes good use of my skills and abilities. (4.2)
- I respect the ability of the person to whom I report. (4.1)

- This organization demonstrates a commitment to workforce diversity. (4.0)
- Employees and management work together to ensure the safest possible working conditions. (4.0)
- The person I report to cares about my job satisfaction. (3.9)
- The person I report to treats me with respect. (3.8)
- The person I report to encourages teamwork. (3.5)
- My work unit works well together. (3.5)

Way down the list of risk factors are fairness of compensation and adequacy of staffing (1.6 and 1.4, respectively). They are risk factors for losing people, but weak ones compared to pride, respect, and teamwork. Of course, organizations must do their best to pay people fairly and staff adequately, but other issues are bigger drivers of workforce retention.

These data show that the factors that make people want to stay in an organization are almost all social – how they interact with their colleagues and how the organization interacts with them. When individuals feel connected to others in the group, they are likely to say yes to requests without needing to know the details, and the group works better. This assertion is not just wishful thinking; it is supported by data and research from inside and outside healthcare.

These data are consistent with the four models for social action described by the German sociologist Max Weber (1864–1920), which are, in essence, four approaches to trying to get people to do things. Weber's four models and my expression of them are shown here:

1. *Tradition.* "This is how we have always done things here."
2. *Aspiration.* "You should do this because it is the right thing to do."
3. *Self-interest.* "You will get a bonus if you do this."
4. *Affection.* "You should do this to keep the respect of your friends and colleagues."

The first three approaches have some effectiveness in motivating people working in healthcare to be at their best, but the fourth is the most reliable by far. If people feel like they really are members of a group, the affection of the other members of the group is something they do not want to lose. Feeling affection leads to building new connections with individual employees, strengthening those connections, and transmitting the right values across those connections – all of which are critical to organizational success.

## Building Connections with Employees

"I've been here 20 years, and I can't remember the last time anyone said hello to me or called me by my name." That comment by a member of the housekeeping staff at a hospital I visited in 2023 captures a problem that managers need to solve. No employee should feel this disconnected from their colleagues or their organization.

Managers should ensure that several types of connections exist for the people reporting to them:

- Bonding connections that strengthen social capital for individuals within the group.
  - The connections between managers and their reports.
  - The connections among members of the groups.

- Bridging connections that strengthen social capital for individuals through relationships outside the group.
  - Connections with colleagues in other parts of the organization.
  - Connections with people doing similar work outside the organization.

Managers should not only make sure every employee who reports to them has genuine connections within the group but also consider how connected each employee is outside the group.

## Strengthening Connections with Employees

Connections get stronger when they are used. An essential basic step for managers is rounding on the people reporting to them. When they round on their reports, they should adopt the same approach to purposeful rounding that nurses increasingly use when doing hourly rounding on hospitalized patients. In fact, at many organizations, managers use technologies developed to support nurse rounding in their interactions with employees.

Structured interactions make the manager–employee relationships more effective. At the Cleveland Clinic, physician annual performance reviews have three parts.

1. Physicians are given feedback on their performance (productivity, quality, and patient experience).
2. Physicians *give* feedback on what would improve the Cleveland Clinic.
3. Physicians and their manager agree on improvement goals for the physician for the year ahead.

These same dynamics should characterize regular interactions between managers and their reports. Managers should give feedback and should receive feedback. And there should be a reliable focus on improvement for the individual and for the group and the organization.

Strengthening the connections among members of the group is important for enhancing the effectiveness of peer pressure and thus activating the "Affection" lever of Max Weber. These interactions also enrich the lives of the individuals and help counter the trends toward social isolation that lead to the *Bowling Alone* problem. Formal meetings help, but informal interactions may matter more.

Redesigns of physical space so that people eat together, hang their coats next to one another, and just naturally spend more time together also contribute to building social capital. For example, NYC Health+Hospitals secured philanthropic funding to create 20 "wellness rooms" across the system. The spaces were designed to be tranquil oases in the bustling hospitals, with soft lighting, soothing music, and fine art. Employees are encouraged to visit them to debrief, release stress, and connect with one another (NYC Health+Hospitals 2024).

## Using Connections with Employees

The connections among individuals working in healthcare organizations represent valuable social capital and should be put to good use. As Nicholas Christakis has pointed out, social capital itself is not inherently good; it could be used for bad purposes as well as noble ones. "The Nazis had tremendous social capital," he said in a recent conversation with me. "They had tremendous transitivity, for example. But look what they did with it."

Among the most important uses of connections is spreading values like respect, teamwork, and the commitment to safety that should characterize the organization's culture. Awareness of these values should be accompanied by understanding that certain behaviors reflect them and should be considered norms – for example, routinely showing respect by saying hello to people by name, sitting down when talking to a patient lying in bed, or thanking members of the housekeeping staff by name after they have cleaned a room.

The phrase "Respect should be as second nature as hand hygiene" is becoming common at many healthcare organizations, as is awareness that there are deeper issues related to respect, such as inclusion and belonging. Values and corresponding behaviors should lead to improved outcomes, and awareness of the organization's performance should help build employees' pride in the organization. Pride enhances their likelihood of staying and of being ready to work flexibly with their colleagues. For managers in healthcare, instilling values and pride is as important as any of their other roles.

# Connections Within and Among Teams

Groups of people have overlapping knowledge; they are smarter than the smartest individual in them, as long as the relationships among the team members allow them to point out each other's blind spots and work together with flexibility. To have teams with such social capital, you need team members who are connected and whose personal social capital grows through membership on the team.

Individuals with more social capital can create teams with more social capital, and the converse is true too. For example, good teams give better care, generate more loyalty from patients, and create more pride for caregivers – and therefore the caregivers want to stay.

## *Building Connections Within Teams*

Within any existing group there are almost always some people who share tight friendships and others who are on the edges of the mini-society. Managers should see it as their job to build connections among those with few or no real relationships and others in the group. For instance, a manager might consider assigning a member with few connections to closely collaborate with a well-connected colleague. Forging connections is a critical step in turning any group into a true team.

Managers should also take responsibility for building bridging connections from the team to other groups with whom they collaborate. For example, emergency department employees should have collaborative relationships with emergency medical service (EMS) teams, both formally and informally. Formal aspects of this relationship should include conveying information about critically ill patients while the ambulance is en route, so that the emergency department staff can be ready.

At Meritus Health in Hagerstown, Maryland, this practice is routine, I found when visiting the facility. Meritus tracks how long "sign-out" of patient information takes after ambulances arrive. Typically, the process takes 16–18 minutes, but at many institutions, it can take a few hours because no one is managing the interaction. Ensuring that this process is done efficiently conveys respect for the time of the EMS personnel, and the EMS personnel tend to return the favor.

When teams are pulled together to address a problem, getting full participation is often a problem, and for a good reason – everyone is already busy with their current job. Leaders should not settle for partial participation, even if nonattendees promise to watch recordings of the meetings or read minutes carefully. Real-time interaction is critical for kicking around new ideas or new ways of working together to address knotty problems. One tactic that often

*Building, Strengthening, and Using Social Capital Connections*

focuses attention and avoids calendar issues is to schedule the team's meetings at a fixed time every week until its work is complete.

## Strengthening Connections Within Teams

Even if connections exist among team members, they may not support ready transmission of important information. For example, teams may not be able to address errors that have been made or steps that should be taken to avoid adverse outcomes. For this reason, it is critical that teams have a culture of psychological safety combined with accountability for addressing problems and making progress toward shared goals.

Teams – and teams of teams – must meet regularly. And they must share performance data that demonstrate how they are doing and whether they are improving.

One striking example of using frequent interaction to create great teams was described to me by my colleague Jessica Dudley, MD, from her tenure as chief medical officer at the Brigham and Women's Hospital Physician Organization. Jessica noted that data on physicians' well-being and professional fulfillment highlighted that one group – palliative care – stood out from the rest in a positive way. When she investigated what they were doing right, she found that the entire team, including social workers and nurses, met every week to discuss every one of their cases. The same dynamic was true for the team caring for HIV patients at the hospital. The leader of that team, Paul Sax,

MD, is nationally prominent for his work in infectious diseases but well known within the hospital for refusing to miss his team's weekly meeting.

The takeaway message: Clinicians in healthcare do love their work and enjoy discussing it. There are a lot of problems in their professional lives to work on, but giving clinicians a chance to spend time together and talk about patients is part of the solution. That cannot be done via email, and virtual or hybrid meetings are not ideal. It is worth noting that the teaching hospital ritual of "morning report," where patients admitted the day before are discussed, moved to virtual formats during the COVID pandemic but is now returning to in-person-only formats at many institutions. In some contexts, getting together in person is just not possible. But when it is, there is no real substitute.

## Using Connections Within Teams

Organizations should concentrate patient volume wherever they have high-performing teams, even if it causes unhappiness with other clinicians who are not members of these teams. It reinforces the effectiveness of the teams, and it improves quality and efficiency. For example, when the City of London decided to concentrate all stroke care at eight hospitals that were designated "hyperacute stroke centers," the result was a decline in mortality and lower costs, even though more patients were surviving (Darzi and Lee 2020). The reason: The higher volume at the eight centers allowed dedicated stroke teams to be available 24/7.

# Connections Within Organizations

The organization has the most important role in creating engagement for the entire workforce, which must be rooted in pride in the organization's mission and values. There are already teams with strong connections within most healthcare organizations, but few organizations have cultivated such teams with high reliability.

## Building Organization-wide Connections

Senior leaders of healthcare organizations should maintain the substrate that encourages individuals to be proud to be part of their organization, which will lower their threshold for becoming engaged members of their teams. To help bond individuals to the organization, leaders must be authentic in conveying values that engage their employees, particularly commitments to safety, to patient-centered care, to a culture of respect, and to teamwork.

Senior leaders should also work to build connections throughout the management organizational chart. The recommendations for frontline managers to round on their reports frequently apply to managers above them, whose direct reports may be other managers. In other words, the organization should create real connections between managers and their supervisors, just as it creates connections between frontline employees and their managers. Organizational alignment is a critical test of whether senior leaders are being successful in creating these connections.

## Strengthening Organization-wide Connections

As is true at other levels, connections at the organizational level become stronger when they are used. Leadership walkrounds are lovely, but no leader can have direct contact with more than a few hundred people on a frequent basis. Therefore, huddles in which people interact in regular short meetings with a well-defined structure turn organizational charts into something akin to living organisms.

The challenge of strengthening connections is particularly important in the complex organizational structures that have emerged through consolidation in healthcare. In these structures, matrixed reporting relationships are becoming the rule, not the exception. While matrixed structures strengthen connections within and among teams, they may create challenges in maintaining connections with the organization as a whole. It behooves C-suite leaders to strengthen their connections with a growing number of reports by employing the same techniques frontline managers use, such as frequent huddles and periodic rounding.

## Using Organization-wide Connections

Organizations should have a reason for being that justifies their demands on employees. Also, organizations need to make that reason known by describing those goals and how they are being pursued. Leaders should be able to articulate the organization's values and identify the behaviors that support those values. Then they should define the norms that will make those behaviors happen reliably. Leaders have many tools at their disposal to get their

*Building, Strengthening, and Using Social Capital Connections*

message out – the organization's communications staff, their own networks of connections within the organization, and the bridging connections they have established with colleagues outside the organization and the community at large.

Brigham and Women's used all those tools to heal the rift that had developed during prolonged negotiations with the nursing union. The day after the contract was signed, the hospital threw an organization-wide celebration – a midday picnic on the expansive hospital lawn bordering Huntington Avenue, one of Boston's busiest streets. The negotiators and press were invited. Several hospital leaders gave short speeches thanking the nurses for bargaining in good faith. Mayor Marty Walsh urged everyone to put aside hard feelings and move on (McCluskey 2016).

Brigham leaders realized that healing would take time and used the bonding and bridging connections they had established over decades to speed the process. The ROI: Within two years, the hospital had achieved nursing magnet status – a recognition of excellent nursing care and the highest honor awarded by the American Nurses Credentialing Center.

Strong and useful connections are powerful instruments of social capital and help teams and networks become even stronger. They build social capital over larger spaces. I discuss both in the next chapters.

# Chapter 4

# Building Teams and Networks in Healthcare

The team is the level where much of the most important social capital in healthcare is created. Networks are where it is distributed and compounded. If you are a manager, your job is to transform the group of employees reporting to you into a real team – people who can work effectively together to achieve their goals – and to encourage the formation of networks to extend your organization's social capital.

Data from patients and healthcare employees demonstrate that teamwork is highly valued by both and is becoming even more valued as medicine becomes more complex. Among employees, data consistently show that perceptions of the quality of teamwork is a major driver of their likelihood of staying with the organization. Among patients, perceptions of how well staff worked together has emerged as the most powerful correlate of overall "likelihood to recommend" by patients in *all* settings – hospital, emergency department, medical practices, clinics, ambulatory surgery, and urgent care.

Hardwiring a culture in which teamwork is a core value takes tremendous effort. Leaders and managers can decide that it is an organizational norm that "we never look like we don't have our act together." For example, some institutions, such as Ohio State University Wexner Medical Center, are working to make doctor-nurse rounding, in which physicians and nurses go into patients' rooms together rather than separately, a norm. That makes it unlikely, if not impossible, for patients to hear different things from different caregivers and then wonder who is wrong.

## Building Great Teams on the Front Lines of Care

Managers are the chief officers for social capital of their team. Their role is to see their reports work as teams and to make those teams great teams. One way to build a great team is to foster real connectedness, both within their team and between their team and the rest of organization.

Real connectedness means relationships characterized by trust, respect, and reciprocity. The goal of such connectedness may seem far-fetched, but there is no harm in asserting the ideal, trying to get as close to it as possible – and *then* pushing to get even closer. Let's use the example of Navy Seal squads, which typically have between 16 and 20 people. As noted in *Team of Teams*, "Beyond such numbers, teams begin to lose the 'oneness' that makes them adaptable[;] . . . communication and trust break down, egos come into conflict, and the chemistry that fueled innovation and agility become destructive" (McChrystal et al. 2015, pp. 126–127). The implication is that within groups of this size, there should be excellent communication and trust, egos should be set aside, and chemistry should fuel innovation.

No one is saying everyone on a team must be friends, and it's worth noting that you do not have to like someone to be glad they are on your team. What is essential is that everyone on the team respect everyone else and acknowledge the contributions they bring. Relationships among team members should be genuine and should be reinforced by regular interactions. And, ideally, their relationships with their colleagues outside the team should be as substantial.

Oxford University psychologist Robin Dunbar has performed extensive research on social connections and has described different levels of relationships. One level is

> casual acquaintances . . . [including] at least some of the people you work with[.] . . . [T]hey are not the sort of people you would go out of your way for; you wouldn't make an effort to have them as part of your more intimate social world[.] . . . [Y]ou might buy them a drink in the pub on occasion, or you might even lend them a book that you didn't mind losing. But you won't be willing to do any favours that involve major costs or risks for you (Dunbar 2021, pp. 26–27).

At a deeper level, Dunbar writes, there is "genuine friendship," which

> shares many similarities with family relationships – except, of course, that we can choose our friends whereas, for better or worse, we have no choice at all over whom we get as family. In many ways, these relationships are all about a sense of obligation and the exchange of favours – the people you wouldn't feel embarrassed about asking for a favour and whom you wouldn't think twice about helping out (pp. 26–27).

Teams in healthcare should be striving to share something beyond "casual acquaintances" that includes characteristics of "genuine friendship." After all, colleagues on a workplace team are not really family members – and some even dislike the use of the word *family* to describe how they should feel about colleagues at work. Of course, while people do get to pick their friends, they do not get to pick whom they work with.

However, given the unpredictability of patients' needs, healthcare teams need aspects of Dunbar's description of friends, such as automatically helping out. That description resonates with my resident telling me, "You never say 'no' to a fellow intern here." Having that dynamic be the norm on healthcare teams may sound ambitious, but it is the right goal.

# Building a Team of Teams

It is hard work to build good teams, and more hard work to get those teams to work together. As Stanley McChrystal noted, Navy Seals are great team players when it comes to their own team, but not so much when they are collaborating with other teams.

Spurred by survey results that indicated only average teamwork across the organization, Vanderbilt University Medical Center (VUMC) decided to build great teams and great teams of teams. To begin, VUMC mounted a pilot project focused on improving the teamwork in one small sector – nurses, environmental services, and food and nutrition services on the Inpatient Orthopedics Unit, a component of the Orthopedics Institute PCC.

The Orthopedics Unit was selected because their leadership had volunteered, not because the unit was experiencing a crisis. But there were enough issues among teams to make the project relevant. For example, there had been some friction between the nurses and the food and nutrition staff. The nurses were often upset because food was not delivered on time. The food service team was unhappy at the nurses for taking their complaints to food service leaders instead of trying to work out their differences with the staff.

As Brian Carlson, vice president of patient experience, described in a paper in *Patient Experience Journal,* VUMC decided to adopt approaches for collaboration across teams that had been effective in other industries (Carlson et al. 2022). Working with external consultants called The Collective Global – again, evidence of "bridging" social capital in the VUMC culture – VUMC followed a structured approach: a "journey in" to gather information, followed by a "journey out" to identify top priorities, and finishing with a "journey to others" to make commitments to other teams.

The three teams were in surprising agreement when asked to name the issues they wanted to work on. All ranked "respect," "relationships," and "communication" at the top of their lists. Over the next several months, they held biweekly team meetings around each of those topics. They explored what was working well, what needed to improve, and what barriers were preventing the teams from achieving change.

The teams adopted a "Hands open, not fists closed" approach that encouraged each team to identify and discuss how it could serve the other teams better before sharing how the other team could help it. The teams discussed what they believed was currently working and what they thought would improve teamwork between the teams. According to Carlson et al. (2022): "The teams ultimately agreed to the commitments and gave each other permission to hold one another accountable to those commitments, to ensure sustainability and the outcomes they all desired" (p. 96).

This work is a great example of how consciously cultivating reciprocity can transform relationships from untrusting to trusting. As Carlson et al. (2022) described:

One of the most impactful commitments was that nurses wanted to be able to trust that environmental services and food and nutrition would follow through on their duties to meet their expectations. Another was that environmental services and food and nutrition wanted to be included, respected, and considered part of the overall team. By including both environmental services and food and nutrition in daily huddles, and having conversations around daily expectations of their efforts, trust was built. Environmental services and food and nutrition began to meet the nurses' expectations, and in return, felt respected and included (p. 96).

The effects were measurable. In subsequent employee-engagement surveys, the team members' responses were more favorable in every survey item. Moreover, the entire Orthopedics Unit saw a significant improvement – from 3.41 to 4.25 on a 5-point scale – in overall staff engagement. Patients also reaped the benefits of stronger teamwork. The unit's overall patient-experience scores climbed from 64.41 to 79.71 over the course of a year.

## Using Meetings to Build Teams

The Vanderbilt project illustrated why frequent meetings are essential in team building – especially in building teams of teams. They provide an opportunity to present performance data on critical metrics to all team members at the same time, to reinforce critical goals, and to create strategies for improvement.

Although frequent meetings make stronger teams, employees might not welcome them. It is up to managers to figure out how to fit meetings in with minimal disruptions to team members' work. One way is to make them brief and efficient, with a structure that is routine and simple. Managers can be confident that they are on the right track when team members insist on having these meetings seven days a week, not just on weekdays. (This has actually happened at many organizations as they get serious about safety.)

While regular 30-minute meetings to review performance are important, so are daily 5- to 10-minute huddles. Those short meetings help keep teams on track. When the Vanderbilt nurses committed to including the environmental services team members in their huddles, the climate changed. Knowing one another's names and roles helped the teams to bond and realize that they had the same mission: to make patients as comfortable as possible.

Managers should see that meetings are conducted in a climate of psychological safety. Amy Edmondson has described that desired state as one in which anyone can speak up about concerns as well as ask questions without looking stupid; ask for feedback without looking incompetent; be respectfully critical without appearing negative; and suggest innovative ideas without being perceived as disruptive (Gallo 2023).

The practice of appreciative inquiry – which focuses on the strengths of individuals, groups, and organizations, instead of their weaknesses – can help motivate teams to work toward goals. For example, a manager can introduce the unit's latest patient-experience score this way: "Our unit's latest score is 65. That's 3 points higher than last quarter. We're on a roll! Now let's figure out what we can we do to score 70 next quarter." Or they can say, "Our unit's latest score is 65. That isn't even close to our goal of 80." In choosing the positive approach managers emphasize their teams' strengths and improvement and turn their focus away from their shortcomings and toward future possibilities (Cooperrider and Srivastva 1987, pp. 129–169).

## Using Meetings to Transmit Information

A goal can be meaningless without data to show why it is important. Yet data can be dry and undigestible. A good rule developed by my colleague Amy Compton-Phillips is: "No data without stories and no stories without data." Everyone on the teams should understand why the metrics are important and why specific areas are focuses for improvement. The stories do not have to be stem-winders; brief statements can do the job. During discussion of the disappointing results of a recent employee-engagement survey for their unit, a team member might explain that they had given a 2 ("I disagree") to the statement "I feel respected" because members of the other teams had never called them by name. In doing so, the team member has brought that metric to life and has effectively identified an issue that needs to be addressed.

My colleagues who work in high reliability are great at running meetings – and at telling stories. In fact, they begin every meeting with a story. Each story has three parts. First, they state the lesson of the story: "I would like to share a message about the importance of speaking up as an advocate for a patient." Second, they deliver the message. Third, they return to the lesson for emphasis: "And that is why it's important that everyone speak up for patients every time." The story is completed within two minutes.

## Using Meetings to Set Behavioral Norms

Meetings are also settings in which managers can establish a team culture that combines psychological safety, accountability, and kindness – the combination advocated in Amy Edmondson's work. Members must feel free to speak up when they see mistakes and to comment without feeling at risk of ridicule or reprisal. At the same time, they should demonstrate that they share in the group's responsibility for performance and that they are not speaking recklessly. Members should understand that their goal is to make the group and other team members better. In that spirit, giving feedback is kind when team members deviate from the norm, and withholding feedback that could support improvement is unkind.

Teammates are likely to adopt the norm because if everyone in the group shares it, the group functions better – and all feel that they are they part of the group. That is the reward for adhering to the norm, and managers must ensure that there is an effective punishment mechanism – in this case feedback – for those who do not adhere to the norm.

As COs for social capital, managers should use the connections within their teams to reinforce behaviors that help the team reach its goals. Without exception, teams in healthcare seek to reduce harm, build trust, and create a culture of respect, especially when they are caring for patients. They need to give patients peace of mind that their problems are understood and appreciated and that everyone is working together on their behalf.

A useful framework called "Compassionate Connected Care" (CCC) was developed in 2014 by Christy Dempsey, the former chief nursing officer at Press Ganey, and is in increasingly wide use by caregivers of all types. Specific themes in CCC for the patient include:

- *Acknowledge suffering*. Caregivers should acknowledge that patients are suffering and show them that they care.
- *Be aware that body language matters*. Body language is as important as the words we use.
- *Address anxiety and uncertainty*. Both are common forms of emotional suffering.
- *Coordinate care*. Patients need to know that their care is coordinated and continuous and that providers are always there for them.
- *Respect patient autonomy*. Autonomy reduces suffering and preserves dignity.
- *Realize the value of caring*. To the patient, real caring transcends delivering medical interventions.

These themes are being used to define behavioral norms on patient care units in organizations adopting CCC. For example, it is standard practice for caregivers to sit at the level of the patient who is in a hospital bed to demonstrate respect or for doctors and nurses to round together so care is coordinated (Dempsey 2021, p. 292).

## Building Social Networks Within the Organization

Healthcare leadership teams and their boards need to give as much energy to managing their social infrastructure as they give to managing their physical infrastructure. Organizations' boards get annual reports on the age and condition of their facilities compared to industry benchmarks; they should get reports on the condition of their organizations' social networks even more frequently. Simply looking at employee turnover rates is akin to trying to monitor quality by tracking hospital mortality or malpractice suits. These approaches are simple and easy, but they are not sensitive enough to monitor what is really going on, let alone drive improvement. Detailed periodic surveys help to pinpoint an issue, such as employees feeling disrespected or disengaged from the work they do. Pulse surveys can measure short-term improvement.

Building strong networks within the organization is one way to increase alignment and engagement organization-wide. Doing so requires enabling employees to interact with each other frequently, both formally and informally.

Formal interactions include all-staff meetings, departmental meetings, and conferences, where employees are likely to learn who is doing what in other parts of the organization. These meetings allow discussions of the group's performance in meeting goals such as efficiency, patient safety, and patient outcomes and experience. At the same time, they convey an important subtext – that everyone in the room is a member of the same team.

Informal interactions, like working on the organization's philanthropic initiative or playing on its softball team, can create social networks almost instantly. And they can also extend social networks beyond the walls of the organization as employees get to know members of other organizations volunteering for the same philanthropy or playing in the same softball league.

Nicholas Christakis (Christakis and Fowler 2011, p. 14) and other social network researchers have shown that the number of connections in a social network are not the only characteristic that matters; the structure of the social network also influences its effectiveness. As noted in Chapter 1, "transitivity" describes the interconnectedness among one's connections.

Tait Shanafelt, chief wellness officer at Stanford Health, shared a great example of transitivity in a conversation we had recently. Shanafelt and his colleagues organized a series of weekend retreats to which about 60 physicians and their spouses/partners were invited. Not everyone wanted to participate, but those who did found that their ties to each other and to Stanford Health were enhanced by their partners knowing their colleagues and their colleagues' partners.

The fact that this social capital–building experiment was successful for those who chose to attend is not surprising. The obvious next question is how to extend the approach to others. For example, there are many physicians at Stanford Health who don't have a partner, and Shanafelt was clear that no one wanted retreats for unattached physicians to be interpreted as singles getaways. Other physicians simply might not have wanted to give any more time to their jobs. But Stanford Health deserves credit for not becoming paralyzed by the exceptions – a syndrome to which we in healthcare are particularly susceptible. Instead, Stanford Health is giving social capital building a try and are convinced they are on to something.

In sum, healthcare leaders need to own the responsibility for strengthening the social networks in their organization and to push that responsibility down to frontline managers. They need to create opportunities for increasing the number and the quality of the connections between managers and the people reporting to them, as well as among those people. Managers should not just be grateful for good connections when they occur; they should work to make connections real and strong for every person on the team. They also should look for ways for their teams to collaborate with other teams in the organization.

# Using Social Networks to Disseminate Values

Activities like weekend retreats build social capital by spreading values, norms, and information, both within and among groups in the organization. Without strong networks, it is hard to disseminate good values throughout the organization. Similarly, good networks without well-conceived efforts to spread the right message do not guarantee the growth of positive social capital. Organizations need both.

What should leaders focus on spreading? They can draw insight from the top correlates of employee engagement from analyses of Press Ganey's 2023 surveys of 2.2 million people in 395 health systems across the United States. In these analyses, "employee engagement" is measured based on responses to survey items that assess employees' connection to and satisfaction with their workplace, their intent to stay, and their likelihood to recommend their employer to potential future employees.

Over the years, our analyses have consistently shown that having more engaged employees, especially nurses, is associated with better safety and clinical outcomes and better patient experience. With lower engagement, the risk of turnover rises; disengaged employees are twice as likely to leave as highly engaged individuals. As every healthcare executive knows, the direct financial costs related to turnover have real impact on the financial bottom line. And for every 1% increase in turnover at hospitals, patient experience scores drop an average of 2 percentile points for overall ratings of care.

If employee engagement really matters, what are its drivers? The types of survey items with the strongest correlation with engagement are:

1. Treating employees with respect
2. Demonstrating that senior management's actions support the organization's mission and values
3. Committing to quality improvement
4. Conducting business in an ethical manner
5. Factoring employees' perspectives into decision making

To the casual observer, these data might seem like a "mom and apple pie" list of aspirations, but they in fact provide valuable guidance on what leaders should focus on as they put the connections of their organizations' social networks to work:

- *Respect.* People want an organizational culture in which respect is as routine and important as hand hygiene.
- *Pride.* People need to feel that their organizations are doing something respected and noble.
- *Trust.* People want to feel confident in the values and the ethics and the effectiveness of the leaders of their organizations.

The reason I repeatedly emphasize respect, pride, and trust is that their impact goes beyond making employees feel good. Figure 4.1 shows the correlation between employees' ratings of whether they feel their organizations treat them with respect and how patients rate the care of those organizations. The striking finding is that when employees felt respected by their organizations, patients rated the organizations highly too.

My Press Ganey colleagues have many, many figures that look a lot like this one, and we have dozens of analyses that tell the same basic story: Good things in the human experience beget more good things in the human experience.

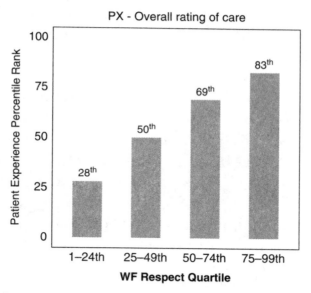

**Figure 4.1** Correlation of workforce ratings on organizational respect with patients' overall rating of care.
PX, Patient Experience; WF, Workforce.
*Source*: Press Ganey, proprietary data.

*Building Teams and Networks in Healthcare*

When employees in healthcare organizations feel more respected, more proud, and more trusting, patients are happier too. And that is because the care is better. It is safer. There is less emotional harm. There really *is* such a thing as excellence, and it begins with caregivers who feel respected, proud, and trusting.

Managers have several overarching tasks before them as social networks are put to work. All these tasks are directed at instilling a culture of respect, pride, and trust.

## Ensuring That Everyone Knows That the Organization Has Good Values

Employees want to feel proud of their organizations. Employee survey data consistently demonstrate that employees' likelihood of staying is strongly correlated with their perceptions of the organization's commitment to values like safety, putting the needs of patients before all else, and treating people with respect. How do they decide what their organizations' values are? The organizations' mission and values should be clearly articulated in signage, on the website, in press releases, and in internal documents.

To paraphrase Ralph Waldo Emerson, every organization is the lengthened shadow of its leaders. Frontline caregivers must be confident that they share their organization's values and that their boss and their boss's boss share those values, as do the bosses above them – all the way to the top of the organization and the board of directors.

When employees internalize the organization's mission and values, they have what experts on workforce social capital call "alignment." It is related to, but different from, "engagement" – an individual's emotional and personal connection to the organization, as influenced by the work environment. Alignment is a critical driver of trust in the organization's leadership and a strong indicator of whether employees intend to stay.

In good times, when an organization is progressing toward its goals, scoring high on patient-experience surveys, and is widely recognized as an asset to its community, alignment is likely to be high. In bad times, alignment is likely to drop. Alignment took a beating during the pandemic as organizations' leaders grappled to ensure the safety of caregivers and patients, were forced to cut services like routine office care and elective surgeries, and had to take drastic steps to deal with what was euphemistically called "financial headwinds." The painful message is that healthcare employees may feel better about healthcare itself than they feel about their own organization and its leaders.

Alignment has also become a bigger challenge as healthcare organizations have consolidated, becoming larger and more complex. The chances that frontline workers feel a personal connection to their chief executives are low today, and it is harder for frontline managers to convey the message to their teams that the chief executive is a good and capable person who can lead the organization toward achieving its goals. Instead, they may toss senior leadership under the bus when dealing with difficult situations, preferring to preserve their sense of solidarity with their teams to building social capital for the organization.

Therefore, a critical use of social networks within organizations is to spread the understanding that leaders have the right values. Of course, that requires that leaders *actually have* the right values – like empathy, respect for others, and trustworthiness – and are perceived as authentic. No one should assume that just because leaders are good people, frontline caregivers will believe it. For example, Harvard Business School professor Frances Frei has written that many high-achieving and data-oriented leaders have difficulty conveying empathy (Frei and Morriss 2020).

Some organizations have started "internal branding" groups within their marketing departments to deal with these situations. These groups study how employees perceive the organization and what it might take to improve that perception. While that might sound manipulative, the fact is that clarifying how organizations and leaders want to be seen – in other words, their brands – helps them understand who they want to be and focus on becoming that organization or leader.

## Seeing That Everyone Knows That the Organization Has Good Goals

Good intentions are not enough to build trust. As Frei and Morriss (2020) described, people also need to know that their leaders have a real plan and that the plan has a good chance of working. And a key step in moving from the fuzziness of good values to the crispness of good plans is having clarity on good goals. In short, people working in healthcare need to understand that the organization has actual measurable goals that must be pursued to live up to the organization's values.

Like an organization's values, its goals should be a source of pride. They also should be big – too big for individuals to control and too big for their teams to accomplish on their own. Goals should be lofty aspirations that can be directly measured, like Zero Harm, reducing the suffering of patients, treating everyone with respect, and improving efficiency so that healthcare can be affordable.

It should be clear that the leaders of the organization care about something beyond achieving a financial margin, because those leaders are inevitably going to be asking employees to change how they work and do things that fall outside of their original job descriptions. Those employees will have one attitude toward such asks if they believe their sacrifices are in pursuit of a big goal; they will have another if they feel like the changes are designed only to achieve a financial margin target. The latter attitude is evident in the increasingly widespread complaint among physicians: "I am just a revenue-generating machine." It is almost surely a driver of the trend toward unionization among doctors.

Our data at Press Ganey show that pride in the quality and patient-centeredness of care matters to everyone in healthcare, not just clinicians. They demonstrate that the most powerful correlate of whether clerks, maintenance workers, and security guards want to stay in an organization is whether they feel that the care their organizations provide is patient centered. The reason: When patients feel like they have received great care, they are thanking everyone on their way out the door. They are saying "You must be so proud to work here." That is not something a security guard is going to hear at many of the non-healthcare businesses where they might work.

Therefore, an important function of social networks within an organization is to hammer home the importance of measurable goals that resonate with the values of the people working there.

## Building a Sense of Belonging

People working in healthcare tend to like when a new neighbor asks, "So where do you work?" That's because there is widespread and well-deserved respect for healthcare and for healthcare organizations. Employees enjoy basking in the glow – if, that is, they feel they belong there. Managers should recognize that respect, inclusion, and belonging lie on a continuum for their employees. Respect should be considered table stakes; every employee should feel that they are being treated with respect. Diversity at all levels ensures that every employee can say "I see someone who looks like me." Inclusion – the knowledge that every voice is not only respected but valued – is a step beyond, and moves employees' engagement to a higher level. And if they feel that they belong in an organization – that they will miss their colleagues who leave and would be missed if they left – then they have a real chance of being great team members.

Building that sense of belonging to a team is an important role for frontline managers. It requires forging the bonding connections within a group. To create an equivalent sense of belonging at an organizational level is a complementary task. The ideal is for employees to feel like they belong on their team *and* that they belong in their organization.

To build a sense of belonging on the organizational level, sharing stories across the organization's social networks can be hugely valuable. These stories should capture the values and show how the organization is living up to them. Yet another reason shared stories are valuable is that everyone knows them. There is a reason that the ancient Greeks developed myths and legends to bind their societies together. Similarly, the local lore of healthcare organizations can help counter the social isolation of the *Bowling Alone* era.

Two of my favorite examples of shared stories come from the Cleveland Clinic during Toby Cosgrove's tenure as chief executive. The first was the widespread common knowledge that he had severe dyslexia. Everyone knew he had almost flunked out of college because he could not pass the foreign language requirement. Everyone knew that he had been turned down by 12 of the 13 medical schools to which he applied. Yes, he eventually became one of the top – if not *the* top – cardiac surgeons in the world. He had had a bumpy start, but he rose above it.

I heard this story from so many people when I visited the Cleveland Clinic. Doctors told me. Nurses told me. Secretaries walking me from one part of the campus to another told me. They all seemed to like the idea of an underdog who had surmounted big challenges only to lead the Cleveland Clinic to the top levels of healthcare. He was *their* underdog, and his success felt like *their* success.

Another example is the now-famous Cleveland Clinic empathy video, developed to rally caregivers around the notion that they should put themselves in the shoes of others. Everyone at the Cleveland Clinic has viewed it, along with more than 7 million others around the world, and, more than a decade later, people continue to allude to a scene at the 1-minute mark and say "I still get choked up when that little girl pets the dog." And whoever they say that to nods and says "Me, too."

This is a shared story that binds people together. The subtext is "We have something in common. We saw the same story. We responded in the same way."

One thing the response to the video makes clear is that patients and caregivers value the same things. Press Ganey's data consistently show that both groups give top priority to safety, to teamwork, to a commitment to quality, to courtesy and respect. If organizations can be highly reliable about pursuing those goals, and are clearly trying to improve, their employees and the public are more likely to be understanding when they occasionally fall short. Therefore, leaders should use the social networks of their organizations to identify what makes their people proud, analyze those data to determine what behaviors are essential to those strengths, and create norms around those behaviors.

In sum, leaders should build social capital by creating cultures of respect, pride, and trust. In doing so, they should convey that the organization's leaders have good values and that the organization has good goals. They should identify the behaviors that bring that greatness to life by turning those behaviors into norms.

They can do this by inculcating behavior norms through teamwork and disseminating them through social networks. Doing so will not require a heavy-handed approach like mandating employees to spread the word. As Christakis and Fowler's (2007, p. 378) research has shown, once people adopt certain values and behave accordingly, those values and behaviors spread throughout their networks.

I have chosen the next case study to conclude this chapter because it demonstrates how achieving good goals can take a real commitment over months and years. It's a lot of work, but the payoff in social capital can be significant.

---

### Case Study 4.1   Community Health Systems: Reducing Harm Across a Large Hospital System

Can large multihospital systems take on quality, safety, and cultural issues? Can they build social capital with bridging connections across dozens of hospitals when that challenge can be daunting even within the walls of a single institution? In a 2023 *NEJM Catalyst* article, Community Health Systems (CHS) described its decade-long journey leading to an 89% reduction in serious safety events (Simon and Van Buren 2023). The

*(continued)*

---

*(continued)*

processes they used and results they achieved demonstrate that social capital can be built at system levels – and that the whole really can be greater than the sum of its parts.

CHS is a for-profit, publicly traded healthcare system headquartered in Franklin, Tennessee, with more than 1,000 sites of care, including 71 hospitals. In 2012, CHS leadership decided to make a serious commitment to improving safety. As Chief Medical Officer Lynn Simon and Chief Safety Officer Terrie Van Buren wrote in 2023, "The catalyst in our journey to zero preventable harm was in analyzing baseline data for serious safety events and recognizing that preventable patient harm was occurring."

In the first year, they took three steps that are examples of social capital building:

1. They created a patient safety organization that included all CHS-affiliated healthcare service providers. This "team of teams" approach provided "bridging connections" within the organization to accelerate learning.

2. They got outside help by partnering with Healthcare Performance Improvement, a consulting group later acquired by Press Ganey. In doing so, they developed bridging connections beyond the walls of the organization.

3. They adopted standardized approaches to measuring safety across the system, exemplifying a bonding connection across the organization.

From the start, CHS leaders agreed on a goal that is widely accepted today but was still somewhat audacious in 2012: Zero Harm. As recently as 2020, my colleague Tejal Gandhi wrote that "*zero* is a controversial term these days in the field of patient safety. . . . [S]ome experts argue that targeting zero is an unnecessary burden to already stressed and overworked clinicians" (Gandhi, Feeley, and Schummers 2020).

Gandhi went on to recall the famous quote from Vince Lombardi, the coach of the National Football League's Green Bay Packers in the 1960s, "Perfection is not attainable. But if we chase perfection, we can catch excellence." Gandhi added, "This is exactly what's occurring in ambitious, forward-looking health systems today. By chasing zero, they are achieving excellence."

Several years earlier, CHS had already decided that Zero Harm was the goal. As their article described:

> Zero preventable harm is possible and is the only acceptable target to align with our core value as a safe and highly reliable organization. Leadership of a zero-harm safety and quality strategic imperative is not only about adopting a safety culture, but also committing that safety must be a core value – one that is constant, unchanging, and unyielding in the face of the latest trends or competing priorities. (Simon and Van Buren 2023)

*(continued)*

*(continued)*

We note these initial decisions because they were important in creating alignment around this work throughout the organization. Frontline caregivers had to believe in the authenticity of leadership's commitment to safety. Having a clear, measurable, and compelling goal that might not be reachable but was a source of pride was a step in the right direction.

Of course, respect for leadership's commitment could have been lost if CHS had not taken steps to pursue that goal. Simon and Van Buren (2023) detail a long series of steps:

- In 2013, CHS instituted practices to keep safety top of mind in all thinking and decision making, such as starting all staff meetings with a safety moment, a two- to four-minute pause to share a near miss, a story, or data.

- In 2013, daily safety huddles were introduced at all levels.

- In 2015, teams began to introduce patient experience, staff engagement, and worker safety information in daily huddles, recognizing that these areas were intertwined with patient safety.

- In 2015, the "Leader Standard Work" table was developed, with detailed descriptions of tasks to be completed to pursue the goal of Zero Harm by three major categories of CHS employees – staff, frontline leaders, and executive leaders. For each of these groups, there are columns for daily, weekly, monthly, and quarterly tasks. This table is too long to be included in this book, but it is a thing of beauty and is provided in full in their *NEJM Catalyst* article. Readers are strongly urged to consider persuading their organizations to adapt and adopt the table.

- In 2016, leaders and staff were trained on the science of human error theory. Leaders were asked "to consistently message that unsafe conditions are not a *bad-people* problem, but rather inherent defects in the design or system that are unable to defend against human error." A framework for responding to three different types of errors – skill based, rule based, and knowledge based – was disseminated.

- In 2017, CHS adopted a state-of-the-art cause-analysis methodology that was used in high-reliability organizations to accelerate learning from safety events.

- In the next several years, CHS began "to expand its zero-harm journey beyond safety and included all-cause patient suffering in the definition of patient harm." Simon and Van Buren's *NEJM Catalyst* article (2023) noted that they had been inspired by the work of my former colleague, Christy Dempsey, then chief nursing officer at Press Ganey, "around the concept of compassionate connected care."

- In 2021, in the midst of the COVID-19 pandemic, CHS introduced service failures – instances when healthcare experiences do not meet patients' expectations – into its high-reliability work.

*(continued)*

*(continued)*

Figure 4.2 shows CHS's steady progress toward the Zero Harm goal.

The results of these years of work were what safety experts expect and hope for. Initially, there was an increase in serious safety events, presumably due to an increase in event reporting. But then the decline began, and went on . . . and on. By 2017, more than an 80% reduction in serious safety events had been achieved.

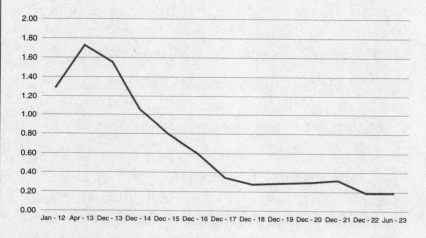

**Figure 4.2**   CHS serious safety event rate over time. X-axis, Month in which events were tabulated; Y-axis, Number of serious safety events per 10,000 patient days. *Source*: Simon and Van Buren (2023). Reprinted with permission of *NEJM Catalyst* (http://catalyst.nejm.org); © Massachusetts Medical Society.

# Chapter 5

# Measuring Social Capital

A ssuming you are convinced that social capital is important and you have insight into what it means for patients and for caregivers, it's time to get to work. How can social capital be measured so that managers can manage it? That is the question I strive to answer in this chapter. I begin with the principles of measuring social capital and then offer a framework with data elements that should be included in any measurement system. I explore the major measurement areas of greatest importance in detail.

## Principles of Measuring Social Capital

The strength of social capital is measured by capturing how people perceive their interactions with others and with the organizational infrastructure where they work or receive care. Asking the right questions shows where and why social capital is strongest or weakest. Combining these data with outcome data – such as safety, quality, productivity, and financial performance – illuminates the power of social capital to drive team and organizational performance.

## *Measuring Social Capital Among Employees*

I begin with social capital among employees for convenience because healthcare organizations have the easiest access to their employees. To measure social capital in the workforce, employee engagement surveys are the starting – but not the ending – point. These surveys offer an array of measures from which to choose, as well as the ability to perform benchmark comparisons with other organizations. The data they provide also support examining performance at different levels and parts of an organization.

Some organizations perform these surveys infrequently – perhaps every two years or so – or not at all. There are several excuses for not doing so:

- "Now is an especially stressful time; we can wait until things get back to normal and are stabilized."
- "It's going to be bad; we don't need numbers to tell us what the problems are."
- "If we measure it and don't do anything about the problems we find, we are going to look like we don't care."

These sentiments are all too human, but not good management. They are analogous to not wanting to measure vital signs or check laboratory data until a patient is doing better. The opposite is the right course. "When patients are sick, hover over them," one of my attendings taught me during my internship. "Don't just do something – stand there."

That approach applies when the workforce is under duress; the right course is to hover over them. "Hovering" in this context means gathering more insights, measuring employee engagement annually, and going deeper on specific issues in specific subgroups through "pulse surveys" – short sets of questions sent at frequent intervals.

Although chief executives and boards may appear to be hovering over employees with frequent surveys, they often rely on single measures – for example, the level of agreement with "I like the work I do" – that address their need to assess current performance and identify problems that need to be prioritized. However, single measures offer minimal help for managers responsible for improving and building social capital. Single measures can tell you that you have a problem, but they don't offer guidance on how to solve it or whether solutions are making a difference.

In addition, single measures assessed for the overall organization can mask serious problems within small parts of the organization. A painful example that played out on front pages of newspapers occurred in 2017 at the Veterans Administration (VA) hospital in Manchester, New Hampshire. This VA had quality ratings – four stars out of a possible five – that placed it in the top third of the entire VA system. In 2016, the Manchester VA ranked above average for both overall patient experience as well as job satisfaction for employees and was one of the top VA hospitals for minimizing the time patients had to wait to see primary care physicians and specialists.

But these good overall metrics may have lulled leaders into overlooking the discontent among a small group of physicians and other employees, who contacted a federal whistle-blower agency and the investigative reporting team of the *Boston Globe* asserting that the hospital had quality problems that were endangering patients. One of the leaders of this group told the *Globe*, "I never thought I would be exposing the system like this. But I went through the system and got nowhere" (Saltzman and Estes 2017).

One lesson from this episode is that overall measures, such as the likelihood of employees to recommend the organization for care or work, are only good starting points, especially when assessed at the organizational level; they are not enough to guide efforts to build social capital. Managers need to understand details, such as whether employees feel respected and involved, if they feel their work supports the mission and values, and the quality of communications and other interactions between people and teams. And they need to understand these data at small units of analysis, like individual patient care units.

As valuable as employee engagement and pulse surveys are, it is important to be ready to go broader and deeper in measurement. "Broader" in this context means exploring issues adjacent to those captured in standard employee engagement surveys – such as safety culture assessment. "Deeper" means using new tools – including AI/natural language processing of narrative data and technology for "listening" to responses from virtual focus groups and crowdsourcing.

Finally, it is worth noting this advice from Michael Porter, who has told me many times in conversation, "If you are going to compete on value, you should think carefully about the unit of analysis at which value is created – and then concentrate your efforts there." Because so much of building social capital occurs at the front lines of care, measurement and analysis needs to be undertaken at that level – in nursing units, medical practices, and emergency departments; in short, wherever teams need to be real teams.

## Measuring Social Capital Among Patients

Similar principles apply to measuring an organization's social capital with patients and consumers. Note here that the goal is assessing the strength of the connections between patients and their healthcare providers and whether these connections are being used to build patients' trust. Hence, the focuses of measurement are on patients' overall confidence in their care, in their perceptions of teamwork and empathy, and on the effectiveness of communication.

Over the years, our analyses have consistently shown that these factors are critical drivers of patients' loyalty to healthcare organizations. However, as is true with employee engagement data, organizations striving for excellence need to look beyond a single "Likelihood to Recommend" measure. Managers need data on aspects of experience that reflect social capital for patients and the organization. For example, managers should understand how much confidence – a surrogate for trust – patients have in their care provider's teams and provider operations, whether they experience caring and compassion, and how they perceive communication among staff.

As is true for employees, going broader and deeper provides information to help build social capital. Tools include measurement of consumer sentiment, AI/natural language processing for patients' comments, and virtual patient and family advisory councils.

Finally, as is true with employees, segmenting patients is essential to get insights into their social capital status and to guide efforts to improve it. Groups of patients defined by race, ethnicity, gender, age, and other factors show important differences in responses to survey items. The goal of management should not be to explain away differences in social capital measures by statistical risk adjustment; the goal should be to build social capital by identifying patients' needs and addressing them.

## Key Measures of Social Capital

In an article in the *Harvard Business Review*, my colleague Nell Buhlman and I discuss findings from patient and workforce surveys (Lee and Buhlman 2024). Table 5.1 contains subsets of items from Press Ganey workforce surveys that are directly relevant to subthemes of social capital. The level of agreement with the statements can be used to assess the strength of social capital in organizations and among teams. Table 5.2 contains items from patient experience surveys. In general, respondents are asked to express their level of agreement with statements on a 1–5 scale. Responses to patient experience questions show whether they recognize the presence or absence of social capital.

**Table 5.1**  Subsets of workplace survey items that are relevant to social capital.

**Staff surveys**

| Employee experience domain | Subtheme | Statements |
|---|---|---|
| | *Indicators of employees' feeling respected and involved* | • This organization treats employees with respect.<br>• My manager treats employees with respect.<br>• This organization cares about employee safety.<br>• Employees' perspectives are factored into decision-making.<br>• Engagement survey results are used to make improvements. |
| Employee engagement | *Indicators of employees' perception of alignment with organization's values* | • Senior management's actions support the organization's values.<br>• This organization cares about quality improvement.<br>• Senior management promotes patient safety.<br>• This organization cares about patients.<br>• The work I do is meaningful. |

*(continued)*

*Measuring Social Capital*

**Table 5.1 (continued)**

**Staff surveys**

| Employee experience domain | Subtheme | Statements |
|---|---|---|
| | *Indicators of collaboration and cohesion* | • Different levels in this organization communicate effectively.<br>• Different units in this organization work effectively together.<br>• My manager encourages teamwork. |
| Diversity, equity, and inclusion | *Indicators of equity and belonging* | • This organization values employees from different backgrounds.<br>• My coworkers value employees from different backgrounds.<br>• My manager treats employees fairly. |

## Staff surveys

| Employee experience domain | Subtheme | Statements |
| --- | --- | --- |
| Safety culture | *Indicators/ measures of safe practices and culture* | • Senior management promotes safety.<br>• Employees can report mistakes without fear.<br>• Employees can raise concerns about workplace safety.<br>• My team discusses error prevention.<br>• Employees can raise workplace safety concerns.<br>• At this organization, there is effective communication among MDs, RNs, and medical personnel.<br>• At this organization, there is effective collaboration between departments.<br>• At this organization, there is effective nurse-physician teamwork.<br>• At this organization, there is effective communication between units. |

*Source:* Press Ganey surveys for engagement, DE&I, and safety culture.

Subset of questions from Press Ganey surveys for engagement; diversity, equity, and inclusion; and safety culture. Unless otherwise stated, respondents indicate the degree to which they agree with each statement on a Likert scale of 1–5.

**Table 5.2**  Subset of items from patient experience surveys.

**Patient and consumer surveys**

| Social capital indicators | Statements |
| --- | --- |
| *Indicators/measures of confidence in care provider, team, and operations* | • I had confidence in the care provider's skill. <br> • Staff worked well together to care for me. <br> • I had access to the practice (via phone or email). <br> • I was able to get an appointment as soon as I wanted. |
| *Indicators/measures of caring and compassionate behaviors* | • Staff care about me as a person. <br> • Staff addressed my emotional needs. <br> • Nurses treated me with courtesy and respect. <br> • Physicians treated me with courtesy and respect. <br> • Care provider showed concern for my questions/worries. |
| *Indicators about communication practices* | • Nurses listened carefully to me. <br> • Nurses kept me informed. <br> • Physicians listened carefully to me. <br> • I was included in decision-making regarding my treatment. |

*Source*: Press Ganey surveys for engagement, DE&I, and safety culture.

Subset of questions from Press Ganey patient experience surveys. Unless otherwise stated, respondents indicate degree of agreement with each statement on a Likert scale of 1–5.

*Social Capital in Healthcare*

For every item, benchmarking is available for subsets defined by demographic data, job category, service line, and so on. Some managers are skeptical of the value of benchmarking, arguing that everyone's goal should be to improve and that the only comparison that matters is whether one is better next year than this year. While the simplicity of this perspective may be attractive, the reality is that the opportunities/imperatives to improve vary among and within organizations. Benchmarking helps identify where managers should focus their attention and stimulates learning.

As noted, much of the real "action" in building social capital occurs at the frontlines of care, and data analysis at those front-line units is often revealing. For example, two neighboring nursing units with similar patient populations can have very different social capital profiles, often reflecting the performance of the managers and changing when the managers change.

At the organizational level and at the front-line unit level, there are consistent correlations among the metrics in Tables 5.1 and 5.2. In addition, Figure 5.1 shows the correlation between patients' likelihood of giving a top recommendation to hospitals and workforce engagement.

The same tight correlation pattern is manifest in Figure 5.2, which shows the relationship between workforce ratings of organizational diversity and equity and three different aspects of patient safety culture.

The high-level conclusion from these analyses is that good things in the human experience beget more good things.

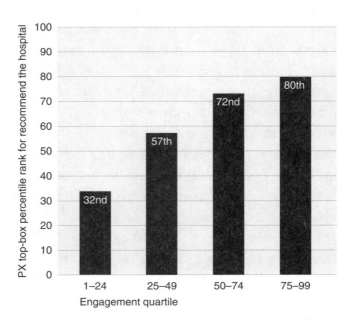

**Figure 5.1** Correlation between hospital workforce engagement and patients' likelihood to recommend the hospital. *Source*: Press Ganey, proprietary data.

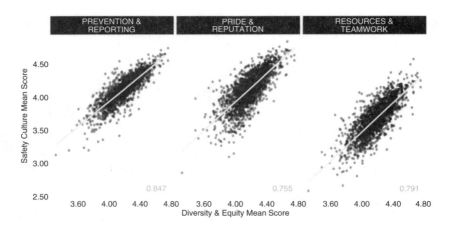

**Figure 5.2** Correlation between organizational diversity and equity scores and measures of safety culture. *Source*: Press Ganey, proprietary data.

*Social Capital in Healthcare*

The more analytic conclusion is that social capital appears to deliver returns on investment via multiple types of performance.

Employee engagement is strongly correlated with the outcomes that really matter to organizations: retention, quality, safety, and patient experience. My colleagues at Press Ganey have studied organizations in the top decile of employee engagement and ranked the statements that are the top 10 drivers of engagement in those organizations:

1. This organization treats employees with respect.
2. My work gives me a feeling of accomplishment.
3. This organization provides high-quality care.
4. This organization cares about quality improvement.
5. Where I work, employees and management work together to ensure the safest possible working conditions.
6. Senior management provides a work climate that promotes patient safety.
7. This organization values employees from different backgrounds.
8. The environment at this organization makes employees in my work unit want to go above and beyond what's expected of them.
9. Senior management's actions support this organization's mission and values.
10. This organization conducts business in an ethical manner.

This analysis and many others that we have performed yield consistent themes, including the importance of a culture of respect, teamwork, and leader behaviors that support an organization's mission and values. All of these themes are tightly tied to employees' trust of their organization, their desire to stay, and their resilience in meeting patients' needs.

## Engagement

Engagement among employees is generally measured by combining responses to several statements, such as these five items:

1. I would stay with this organization if offered a similar position elsewhere.
2. I would like to be working at this organization three years from now.
3. I feel like I belong in this organization.
4. I would recommend this organization as a good place to work.
5. Overall, I am a satisfied employee.

Responses are scored on a 1–5 scale and then averaged.

Figure 5.3 shows the distribution of employee engagement scores for organizations surveyed by Press Ganey from 2018 to 2024, with numbers in the middle representing medians and the top and bottom numbers representing the 90th and 10th percentiles, respectively. (The data are

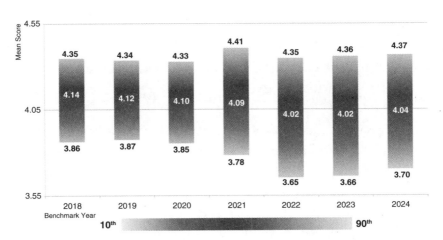

**Figure 5.3** Median and 10th–90th percentiles for employee engagement by year.
*Source*: Press Ganey, proprietary data.

based on one- to two-year "look-backs," so 2022 reflects employee experiences in 2021.)

Figure 5.3 is worth pondering. Note that as the COVID pandemic hit, the median went down and now has started to come up. But note also that the gap between the best and worst organizations increased dramatically. The difference between the 10th and 90th percentiles went from 0.48 in 2020 to 0.70 in 2022.

Engagement at the stronger organizations got stronger, while it fell markedly in the weaker organizations. The edge of the 90th percentile went from 4.33 in 2020, before the pandemic, to 4.37 in 2024, after the pandemic; this means that the best got better throughout the crisis. In

*Measuring Social Capital*

contrast, the weakest 10th percentile had something like a collapse. More recently, in 2023 and 2024, the weaker organizations are starting to improve, but they are still well below pre-pandemic levels.

Similar patterns are found in analyses of alignment, which is related to engagement, but more personal. Alignment is directly tied to employees' confidence that leadership's values resonate with theirs and their confidence that their voices are heard and considered. Alignment is deeply tied to trust in the leaders of the organization.

As an example of how alignment is measured, six statements can be used to measure alignment for physicians:

1. I can easily communicate any ideas and/or concerns I may have to hospital administration.
2. I have adequate input into decisions that affect how I practice medicine.
3. I have confidence in senior management's leadership.
4. Hospital administration is responsive to feedback from physicians.
5. Overall, I am satisfied with the performance of clinic administration.
6. This hospital treats physicians with respect.

Agreement with statements on engagement and alignment correlate strongly with employees' likelihood of staying in the organization, with the organization's safety culture, and with patients' experience. Overall, agreement with both fell during the pandemic, then leveled off, and are now starting to improve. And they both showed a spreading of the pack with a widening gap between the 10th and the 90th percentiles.

But agreement with statements indicating engagement has consistently been higher than with statements signifying alignment in our surveys. This observation suggests that many employees feel better about their organizations than they do about their leaders and that working on alignment should be a specific focus for leaders.

## *Respect*

For patients and for employees, respect is a "must have." Press Ganey data demonstrate that, if people in either group do not feel respected, connections to the organization are weak. It is necessary (although not sufficient) to earn trust. This conclusion is hardly surprising, but the consistency of the findings across various types of human experience is impressive:

- Among the top decile of healthcare providers in terms of employee engagement, the most powerful single driver is "This organization treats employees with respect."
- When employees indicate that they agree or strongly agree with the organizational respect statement, 84% are engaged or highly engaged.

- When employees say they disagree or strongly disagree with the organization respect statement, 50% are disengaged, and another 41% are neutral.

- When employees give a negative response to the organizational respect statement, their risk of leaving increases 7.6-fold.

- When patients give a high likelihood of recommending the providers of their care, they almost always report that they were treated with courtesy and respect.

Employees in different job categories report markedly different experiences with organizational respect. At the top are senior managers (4.57 on a 5-point scale) and other managers (4.23). The average rating from 61,000 physicians surveyed by Press Ganey was 3.92, and the average among 228,727 nurses was 3.87.

Using artificial intelligence and natural language processing, researchers can measure variations among different subsets of people in greater depth. My colleagues at Press Ganey explored this issue in a data set of 1,307,783 open-ended comments written by patients in 1,917,103 patient experience surveys in 2020 and 2021. A representative sampling of the comments can be found in Table 5.3.

The Press Ganey team found that respect-related themes appeared in 26% of all positive insights about physicians and 32% of all positive insights about nurses, making respect the most frequently mentioned positive experience for patients. Negative experiences about respect were mentioned less often – in 10% of all negative insights about physicians and 16% of all negative insights about nurses.

**Table 5.3** Open-ended comments about respect from patient experience surveys, 2020–2021.

| Positive and negative comments about respect | |
| --- | --- |
| **Positive comments** | **Negative comments** |
| The doctor was very understanding and listened and [was] helpful. | [T]he doctor I couldn't understand, she acted like she didn't care, wouldn't explain what they were doing or what [the] results were. |
| She's a doctor, a woman of heart and understanding; she's trusting and caring. | When he said to me, "It is what it is," I felt that he didn't care about my welfare, being an African American or being a woman due to the manner of throwing his arms and looking directly at me (scary for me)! |
| [Doctor] was very patient and provided an understandable explanation. | One doctor in ER did not give me time to explain something and was rude. |
| Whenever I needed to be walked to the bathroom, [nurses] escorted me and were kind and treated me with dignity and made sure I was safe. | When I was having a breathing problem after getting out of ICU, the nurse didn't believe me and was mean and rude. |

*Source*: Press Ganey, proprietary data.

In both inpatient and ambulatory settings, patients who self-identified as Black had higher rates of comments, both positive and negative, about respect than patients who identified as White. This difference suggests that Black patients may be more attuned to caregiver behaviors that show or fail to show respect.

In sum, respect consistently emerges as an important prerequisite to strong connections between patients and caregivers and among caregivers. While no one comes to work intending to show disrespect, vast numbers of patients and employees feel less than respected. Respect can be measured, and it can be improved.

## Quality, Safety, and Reliability

For both employees and patients, data consistently demonstrate that trust in healthcare organizations requires commitment to safety and the goal of Zero Harm. The following statements appear among the top 10 strongest drivers of engagement in top-decile organizations:

- This organization provides high-quality care.
- This organization cares about quality improvement.
- Where I work, employees and management work together to ensure the safest possible working conditions.
- Senior management provides a work climate that promotes patient safety.

For patients, any inkling that their care may not be safe destroys their trust. Figure 5.4 shows how safety concerns

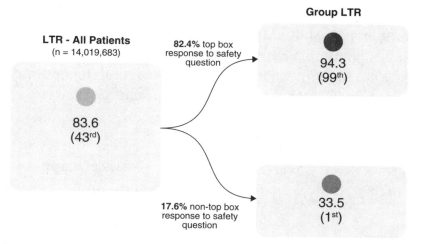

**Figure 5.4** Impact of safety concerns on patients' likelihood to recommend their caregivers.
LTR = likelihood to recommend.
*Source*: Press Ganey, proprietary data.

correlated with trust in a subset of 14 million ambulatory patients during the latter phases of the COVID pandemic. Overall, 83.6% of these patients gave a top rating to their providers, which placed this subset at the 43rd percentile of Press Ganey's national data set. However, among the 17.6% of patients who had a safety concern, only a third gave a top likelihood-to-recommend rating to the practice, which put them in the first percentile.

An additional analysis of the subset of patients who gave their physician a top rating, the likelihood to recommend, was only in the second percentile if there was a safety concern. In short, safety concerns create a trust hole that providers cannot dig out of. In contrast, clear commitment to high reliability principles wins the loyalty of both patients and providers.

Given the importance of safety to patients and employees, senior leaders should track employee data relevant to safety culture. Figure 5.5 shows specific items from Press Ganey's safety culture survey and the improvement that occurred in most of them over the last year in our entire database.

## Teamwork

Teamwork is yet another currency of social capital that is highly valued by both patients and employees. For

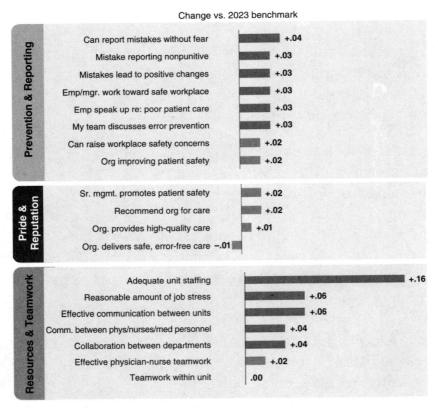

**Figure 5.5** Safety culture items and changes from 2023 to 2024.

*Source*: Press Ganey, proprietary data.

patients, evidence of good teamwork is the top correlate of overall likelihood to recommend in every care setting. For employees, as noted elsewhere, low levels of agreement with the statement "My work unit works well together" is a 3.5-fold risk factor for employees being interested in leaving. And, as we found, one of the most important drivers of engagement at top-decile organizations is a positive response to the statement "The environment at this organization makes employees in my work unit want to go above and beyond what's expected of them." In short, employees not only want to be on good teams; they want to be on *great* teams.

That desire is why social capital in general and teamwork in particular are unifying forces for healthcare improvement and should be at the core of organizational strategy. The items in the safety culture survey shown in Figure 5.5 include several that can help leaders assess teamwork, and it is important that these data be collected and analyzed at the frontline team level. Managers should also consider patients' assessment of teamwork from patient experience surveys and explore the impact of interventions that make teamwork more transparent to patients, such as doctors and nurses rounding together.

## *Leader Behaviors*

Measuring leaders' behavior is sometimes a touchy topic; leaders usually know that they are working relentlessly for the good of their organizations, and it is difficult for them to believe that others are not aware of the values that guide them. Many leaders are uncomfortable putting their emotional investment in the work of healthcare on display. But the fact is that, as organizations have become bigger and more complex, only a small percentage of employees can really have direct contact with the chief executive or other senior leaders. For that reason, it is critical that leaders use every opportunity to convey to employees that their values are good and authentic.

The items listed in Table 5.1 that capture employees' alignment with their leaders provide insight into what drives trustworthiness for frontline caregivers. These items include:

- Senior management's actions support the organization's values.
- This organization cares about quality improvement.
- Senior management promotes patient safety.
- This organization cares about patients.

The averages for these items tend to be in the range of 3.5 to –3.9 on a 5-point scale. No real leader should be happy with just being average on these metrics; the real goal is 5.0. Leaders should swallow hard and use these measures on a regular basis.

## Analyzing Data at Different Organizational Levels

Another useful way of analyzing data from employee engagement surveys is at the organizational level. Table 5.4 shows measures in the core items of Press Ganey's

**Table 5.4**  Employee engagement items relevant to different organizational levels.

| Press Ganey employee engagement core items relevant to organization, manager, and team | |
|---|---|
| | **Core items** |
| Organization | • I get the tools and resources I need to do my job well.<br>• This organization provides career development opportunities.<br>• This organization cares about employee safety.<br>• This organization supports me in balancing my work and personal life.<br>• I have confidence in senior management's leadership. |
| Manager | • The person I report to encourages teamwork.<br>• The person I report to is a good communicator.<br>• The person I report to gives me useful feedback.<br>• The person I report to treats me with respect. |
| Team | • My work unit provides high-quality care and service.<br>• My work unit works well together.<br>• I enjoy working with my coworkers.<br>• There is a climate of trust within my work unit. |

employee engagement relevant to the overall organization, managers, and teams.

In summary, engagement surveys are effective tools to measure the strength of social capital among the workforce, and patient experience surveys can provide additional perspective on teamwork and the extent to which an organization has a culture of respect. Overall measures, such as likelihood to recommend the organization for care or likelihood to recommend it for work, are good starting points. But managers/leaders should dive deeper and look at responses and trends on individual items that evaluate the strength of the bonds between people both within teams and between employees and the organization.

The data should be analyzed from multiple perspectives – team, unit, role, and respondent demographics. Responses to questions that ask about how employees are treated – if they feel their work supports the organization's mission and values and how they judge the quality of communications and interactions between people and teams – warrant particular attention. Declining scores for these items signal erosion in relationships between team members, which can negatively impact teamwork and, by extension, outcomes of care.

# Chapter 6

# Social Capital as the Core of Healthcare Strategy

The changing nature of healthcare has made leadership in healthcare harder today than it has ever been. Every type of organization in the healthcare system is under duress – providers, payers, and vendors. No one out there is having an easy time of it.

Most leaders now suspect that there will be no return to "normalcy." If they are correct, it is critical to think more deeply about why things have become so difficult and what responses are most likely to be effective.

My discussion here draws on the work of Harvard Business School's Michael Porter, whose seminal work began well before I started collaborating with him two decades ago. Porter's Five Forces framework explains why competitive threats for healthcare organizations have become so intense today and will only get more intense in the future.

## The Five Forces That Should Shape Strategy

As Porter (2008) has suggested, leaders frequently define *competition* too narrowly. They focus on their direct

**149**

competitors – rivals that perform the same services, hire the same types of personnel, and so forth. Hospitals focus on other hospitals. Insurers focus on other insurers. Doctor groups focus on other doctor groups.

But Porter pointed out that the competition for profits goes beyond these industry rivals and includes four other competitive forces: *customers, suppliers, potential new entrants,* and *substitute products.* For example, if an organization's customers have complete control over what price they will pay, it will be difficult to achieve a financial margin. Similarly, if the suppliers of essential goods needed by the organization have a monopoly, they can raise their prices, again compromising the ability of the organization to make a profit. If the price of entry into the market is low, new entrants can start competing for revenue. And if customers can meet their needs in other ways, that too becomes a threat (Porter, 2008).

For virtually all healthcare organizations, recent changes have intensified pressures from the Five Forces. Depending on where your organization sits in the healthcare system, the landscape may be described differently, but most organizations feel stressed in their ability to extract the profit margins that they believe they need to thrive – or to extract any profit at all. For virtually all organizations, there has been consolidation among their customers and suppliers. New entrants are coming after parts of their business that yield a profit while avoiding the parts that do not.

For example, most U.S. healthcare providers are heavily dependent on revenue from the growing percentage of patients covered by the government-sponsored health plans Medicare and Medicaid. The good news is that, due to the Affordable Care Act, a lower percentage of Americans are uninsured.

However, providers have very limited ability to influence payment rates for Medicare and Medicaid patients, and most provider organizations find that their revenue for these patients falls well below their fully loaded costs – costs that take into account the organization's overhead, including the costs of maintaining its infrastructure, administration, and other personnel costs. These overhead costs exist for a hospital even if a bed lies empty. Marginal costs are the increased expenses that result from admitting a patient to that bed, like the costs of providing food and medications for that patient. Patients covered by Medicare or Medicaid often bring revenue that is greater than the marginal costs but lower than the fully loaded costs. Thus, it is better financially for hospitals to have a patient in that bed than to have it empty, but if *all* its beds are occupied by Medicare or Medicaid patients, the hospitals will not be able to maintain their facilities or pay their employees.

Many healthcare providers have covered these losses by cost shifting, often by negotiating higher payment rates from the commercial insurers that provide coverage for people who get insurance through their employers or purchase insurance on their own. However, this "escape route" has been closing, as there has also been consolidation among private insurers. The commercial marketplace is increasingly dominated by national for-profit megaplans, such as United, Aetna, Cigna, and Humana. The market power of these consolidated purchasers makes it hard for providers to walk away in any negotiation.

Adding to pressures from purchasers of care, there has been consolidation and shortages among suppliers. As a result, providers have trouble getting medical staff and critical medications. They have to do what it takes to keep the lights on – and frequently that means paying higher costs.

In contract negotiations with insurance plans, healthcare providers explain that they have had to increase what they are paying nurses, add physicians to address the greater complexity of state-of-the-science medicine, and raise wages for support staff to keep them from leaving for other industries. Healthcare providers note that the costs they are paying for pharmaceuticals and other essential supplies have gone up as well.

But when healthcare providers then demand increases of 6 to 10%, or even more, commercial insurers balk. They have their own version of the Five Forces playing out. *Their* purchasers are employers, who want to keep their healthcare costs flat and would settle for increases of just a few percentage points.

Meanwhile, the competitive threat from new entrants has intensified for both providers of healthcare and insurers. New entrants include start-up companies that provide services like urgent care and virtual medical care, but also include existing businesses extending their reach by providing healthcare services. For example, Amazon Prime members can sign up to be One Medical patients for $9.00 per month and get access to 24/7 virtual care consultations.

That was Amazon Prime's offering in the autumn of 2024; it is almost certain that other offerings will be on the table within several months, as major retailers keep experimenting with new models for delivering healthcare. Frequently these new models do not work financially and/or fail to attract enough patients. Walmart, for example, announced in April 2024 that it was closing all 51 of the health centers in Walmart stores and shutting down its virtual care operation. Its announcement said: "This is a difficult decision. . . . [T]he challenging reimbursement environment and escalating operating costs create a lack of profitability that make the care business unsustainable for us at this time" (Walmart, 2024).

The retreat from healthcare by Walmart and some other retailers does not mean they won't be back, however. These businesses must seek other revenue streams as they struggle with their own versions of the Five Forces. Startups wither away and big ventures by non-healthcare companies fail, but healthcare is such a huge part of the economy that nontraditional competitors will keep coming back and exert pressure on healthcare providers to adapt.

Another dynamic contributing to Five Forces pressures is rival organizations' increasing likelihood to buy market share by offering prices well below the fully loaded costs

*Social Capital as the Core of Healthcare Strategy*

of their competitors. The health insurance plans or other organizations that currently have the customers are loath to drop their prices, since they need to spread their overhead costs over as many patients or health plan members as possible. But for the rival seeking to take the business away, it makes sense to offer a very low price, provided it is greater than the new marginal costs.

This kind of price war is great for consumers, of course, but stressful for organizations trying to hold on to their customers and their profits. That stress is, in theory, good for society, since it forces rivals to push constantly for ways to become more efficient and more attractive to their customers. But in a world in which geographical location matters less and many services can be delivered anywhere electronically, this dynamic means that competitive pressures have become relentless from every angle.

In essence, if your organization is making a profit on any of its activities, someone is coming after it. The Five Forces play out differently for different types of organization, but the intensity of the threat of competition is increasing for virtually all.

If you are starting a new business, you should think about the Five Forces before committing to go forward so you know what you are getting into. But if you are already in healthcare, you probably don't have the option of leaving.

You can't get overwhelmed. You need to plot a path forward. You need a strategy. And that strategy inevitably leads to building social capital.

# Strategy as the Antidote to Competition

One of Michael Porter's famous teachings is that "strategy is the antidote to competition." His message was that you cannot outwork or outrun the Five Forces, and you cannot deal with them by merging with everyone in sight, thus eliminating competition from rivals – and violating anti-trust regulations. Instead, organizations must use strategy to differentiate themselves from their competition.

Porter and I wrote an article called "Why Strategy Matters Now" in the *New England Journal of Medicine* in 2015, which began with the distinction between "operational effectiveness" and "strategy" (Porter and Lee 2015, p. 1881). Operational effectiveness means doing a better job at what you do. It means hiring good people, working hard, adopting best practices, improving efficiency, and reducing errors and harm.

In the second half of the 20th century, when healthcare cost less than today and the U.S. economy was more robust, operational effectiveness was almost always enough to guarantee business viability. But as funding has become tighter in healthcare and expenses have increased, something more than doing a good job has become necessary to thrive: strategy.

## Strategy Requires Making Choices

A key aim of our 2015 article was to clarify the distinction between operational effectiveness and strategy. If operational effectiveness is about improving what you do, strategy is about making *choices* about what you do.

Choices are hard. When I listened to Porter describe how choices were inherent to strategy, I recognized that I – along with many of my colleagues in healthcare – didn't really like to make choices. When you make choices, you make someone angry. And my colleagues and I tend to be nice people who are conflict-averse, and we would rather not anger our friends.

Of course, one thing even worse than angering friends is leading one's organization into failure. Asked whether we would rather be in an organization that can make choices or one that cannot, most of us recognize that the former is better than the latter. Porter would often say, "You can't do everything for everyone the same way as everyone else." You must make choices – and then do a great job at the things you choose to emphasize.

How do you choose what to do? You certainly don't want to make choices based on politics – listening to whomever talks the loudest or whomever is your closest friend. And you shouldn't make your choices based on what work is most profitable under the current reimbursement system, because someone – a new payer, supplier, entrant, or rival – is going to come after those profits.

Strategy requires making choices based on two simple questions:

1. *What are you seeking to do for whom?* In other words, who is your customer, and what value are you creating for that customer? How are you creating value –

in other words, how are you making life better for that customer?

**2.** *How are you going to be different?* Porter pointed out that if you are indistinguishable from your rivals, you will end up in a price war and have difficulty making a financial margin. Every organization, both for-profit and nonprofit, has to make a margin in order to invest for the future and thrive.

Organizations do not have to do every activity in the value chain; whatever organization can deliver care most efficiently or conveniently to the patient should have the role. For example, where patients once relied on their primary care providers to vaccinate them, they now routinely head to the nearest pharmacy for flu shots, COVID boosters, and any of the increasing array of recommended immunizations. This has become a win/win/win/win situation. Patients don't have to leave their neighborhoods. Hospitals and clinics are relieved of having to acquire and store supplies of vaccines. Insurers have fewer organizations to bargain with. Pharmacies have increased revenue. However, patients still tend to look to their providers for advice on which immunizations to get.

Managing rather than monopolizing the activities in the value chain is what makes an organization stand out from rivals. In fact, the ability to partner with outsiders like pharmacy chains could become an important differentiator. In other words, competitive differentiation could come from the social capital involved in building bridging connections.

*Social Capital as the Core of Healthcare Strategy*

## Strategy Requires Competitive Differentiation

The second key question that should guide strategic choices, "How are you going to be different?," is addressed in the article that Michael Porter and I wrote in the *Harvard Business Review* entitled "The Strategy That Will Fix Health Care" (Porter and Lee 2013). In this paper, we laid out six intertwined components of a strategy for improving value in healthcare.

The six components of the framework can be translated into terms that make them recognizable as currencies of social capital. Overall, the framework emphasizes the need for:

1. Teamwork
2. Measuring outcomes that matter to patients, as well as the costs of delivering those outcomes
3. Use of financial and nonfinancial incentives that reward progress in improving value
4. Delivering excellent care across episodes that are meaningful to patients rather than just during transactions that are reimbursed by fee-for-service payment
5. Extending high-value and high-reliability care across systems that cover regions
6. Use of information technology systems that support these goals

> **Case Study 6.1  The Vanderbilt Experience: Using a Social Capital Strategy to Gain a Competitive Edge**
>
> Over three decades, Vanderbilt University Medical Center (VUMC) has systematically adopted the strategies outlined in this chapter. In doing so, it has cultivated bonding connections in building teamwork and bridging connections through demanding, but rewarding, "team of teams" work to respond to the increasing pressures on healthcare. It has modified its leadership and governance structures to support care organized around groups of patients with shared needs. And it has found creative solutions to bundling payments. The following sections detail Vanderbilt's steady progress to a sustainable return on investment.

## *Creating Integrated Practice Units*

The first of the six components in Porter's and my framework invokes the term *integrated practice unit* (IPU), which refers to a tightly integrated multidisciplinary team focused on patients with a specific medical condition (Porter and Lee 2021). Patient care has long been organized around specialty departments and divisions such as surgery, cardiology, and oncology – a structure that makes sense in training physicians and when the dominant priority is optimizing the ability of physicians to do their work. That physician-centric approach also made sense when the payment system was based nearly completely on fees for services performed by physicians and when medicine itself was less advanced.

Today, however, medicine is far more complex and costly than in the past century, and delivering state-of-the-science care often requires deep collaboration among clinicians in different disciplines. Although physicians have always collaborated with each other, teamwork hasn't been the top priority in determining how academic medical centers are organized. Patients would be admitted to the hospital with an array of issues, and the admitting physician would call for consultations in cardiology, nephrology, neurology, and so on. Whoever was the attending physician on those services would show up.

The attending physicians might be well trained in their fields, but their expertise might not overlap perfectly with the patient's problems. For example, I was trained in cardiology, but some of my cardiology colleagues plunged into the interface of oncology and cardiology. They do almost all their clinical work at the cancer center next door to my hospital, and they know far more than I do about the cardiac complications of cancer treatments and the cardiovascular problems that various cancers can cause.

Being an expert involves more than knowledge; deep experience brings judgment. Researchers who have studied the question of "What makes an expert?" have concluded that there is no substitute for learning over time. K. Anders Ericsson studied musicians and concluded that "even the most gifted performers need a minimum of 10 years (or

10,000 hours) of intense training before they win international competitions" (Ericsson et al. 2007). The experts I respect most in clinical medicine tend to agree. Even when I know the same facts as colleagues who are more deeply immersed in an area, they are better able to sense when the textbook descriptions might not apply and something unusual is happening.

Experienced clinicians are also more comfortable living with uncertainty. They might not know exactly what is causing a patient's problems, but they can tell when watching and waiting is a reasonable next step. They can provide reassurance by saying "I don't know what you have, but I have seen almost every bad thing that can happen, and I don't think any of those things is going on with you."

The ideal is a team with deep experience with their patients' conditions and with each other.. Teams with clinicians who know what to expect from each other. Teams with social capital. IPUs can be considered the gold standard of integrated care for targeted patient conditions.

VUMC was in the vanguard of the IPU movement. The care center model bubbled up at Vanderbilt from frontline clinicians who were pained to see their patients bounce around in the system. In 1997, the Vanderbilt Asthma, Sinus and Allergy Program (VASAP) was started by a group of physicians who took care of patients with respiratory symptoms like coughing, wheezing, runny noses, and headaches – symptoms that could be due to asthma (a lung disorder), hay fever (an allergy disorder), or chronic sinus infections (a focus for ear, nose, and throat physicians).

Frequently, patients with these symptoms would be referred to a specialist in one of these areas, only to be told they really needed to see someone in another area.

Four of the specialists in these areas decided they should start seeing patients in one building, which would also house radiology services to do x-rays and CT scans and technicians to do allergy testing and pulmonary-function evaluations. This clinic was among the first at Vanderbilt to implement electronic medical records, and nurse practitioners were at the front lines of care.

The specialists' motivation was simple and noble – they felt that it was the decent thing to do for their patients. One of these specialists, an allergist named S. Bobo Tanner, told me, "These are working people who often drive two hours to get to us. We didn't want them to have to make that drive over and over and pay their copayments more than once."

That said, VASAP didn't fit smoothly with the traditional organizational structure and the flow of revenue through departments defined by physician specialty. However, department chairs grudgingly went along, and, like many early IPUs, VASAP survived because of the stubbornness of its physician leaders and constant support from the central administration.

By 2009, the VASAP model had spread and Vanderbilt's leaders began exploring how to make team-based care a competitive differentiator. The new vice chancellor for health affairs, Jeff Balser, MD, had both the bonding and the bridging social capital to advance this agenda. He was

*Social Capital in Healthcare*

a 1990 graduate of Vanderbilt's MD/PhD program, and, after training at Johns Hopkins, he returned in 1998 to play leadership roles both in research and care delivery. At the start of his tenure as vice chancellor, he helped lead VUMC through a deep financial crisis. He had earned the thick trust of his colleagues at VUMC through a wide range of experiences over many years.

IPUs like the Orthopedics Institute, with a scope that was contained in a single department, were led by their department chairs. In other cases, where service lines crossed departments – for example, cancer and cardiovascular disease – the health system assumed responsibility for their management. In the latter cases, those centers had a tripartite leadership structure, with an executive medical director (a physician), a chief nursing officer, and a chief administrator. All three of these individuals were appointed by the health system, and there was poor buy-in from the clinical departments.

Balser knew he had to work out a system for resolving the conflicts among department chairs and physicians working across disciplines by developing a system for managing IPUs that was agreeable to everyone. He and his colleagues enlisted Porter's advice in redeveloping Vanderbilt's versions of IPUs, which had been renamed patient care centers (PCCs).

## Providing Incentives to Change

By 2012, Balser and his colleagues realized that they needed a new management structure and moved to what they called "PCC 2.0." A key change was that each PCC executive medical director would be appointed or removed and annually reviewed by the chairs of all departments with faculty participating in the PCC. In addition, to ensure that the PCC's work was aligned with those of the other stakeholders of the medical center, each PCC would have an executive committee that included the same department chairs as well as the relevant hospital and clinic presidents. Dr. Wright Pinson, VUMC's deputy chief executive and chief health system officer, led the process of establishing this new governance and accountability structure and attended many of the executive committee meetings as the new structure was launched.

By 2024, there were 21 PCCs in addition to 16 care support centers (CSCs) with analogous governance structures to provide laboratory and imaging services. Management of each PCC and CSC had incentive compensation goals that aligned closely with those of the relevant department chairs and hospital and clinic leaders. These incentive goals were reviewed quarterly in PCC "goalfests," where performance data below budgeted levels were made visible and discussed in a group setting with all PCC leaders present.

## Bundling Payments

PCCs deliver an entire care episode – for example, diagnostic tests, surgery, and rehabilitation therapy for a hip replacement – at one facility, and they are reimbursed with a bundled payment – a single payment for a "bundle" of services. Bundling payments streamlines healthcare providers' accounting and billing and reduces the number of copayments for patients. The VUMC recognizes a return on investment on its social capital through its ability to respond to increasing numbers of bundled payment initiatives. At the federal level, the Centers for Medicare and Medicaid Services continues to test different iterations of its initial bundled payment model, the Bundled Payments for Care Improvement. In addition, a goal of Tennessee's Medicaid's Health Care Innovation Initiative is to push the state's Medicaid managed-care organizations away from fee for service by implementing 75 bundled payments for complete episodes of care for different conditions.

VUMC was unusual among academic medical centers in being ready to explore new payment models. Anticipating the trend toward risk-based bundled payments, VUMC established a dedicated Episodes of Care team to drive performance under these payment models. Originally under the nursing leadership of Brittany Cunningham, the team subsequently evolved to include a physician-nurse dyad leadership model.

The physician leader, C. J. Stimson, graduated from medical school and law school and completed his residency in urology at Vanderbilt. Then, like Balser, he went to Johns Hopkins for more training. While there, Stimson worked at the Center for Medicare and Medicaid Innovation and helped define the payment model specifications for federal bundled-payment programs.

When he returned to Vanderbilt, Stimson joined the Episodes of Care team as the medical director to focus on maximizing VUMC's performance in Medicare bundled-payment

*Social Capital as the Core of Healthcare Strategy*

models. Vanderbilt's early experience in health system operations, change management, and bundled payments validated the thesis at the core of Porter's value-based care paradigm – that a more rational alignment between payments and outcomes can deliver higher value care to all healthcare stakeholders. It was clear to Stimson and his VUMC leadership colleagues that the next evolution in bundled payments would expand the value proposition beyond the Medicare population to commercially insured patients and would do so from the provider rather than the payer perspective.

In short, Vanderbilt decided that it would push the bundled payment agenda even if commercial payers dragged their feet. VUMC had enough confidence in its ability to capitalize on teamwork and a commitment to high-value care that it would get out in front of the market.

VUMC's Medicare experience allowed Stimson and the Episode of Care team to develop and execute a commercial bundles program called MyHealth Bundles. When commercial payers were antagonistic to a provider-led commercial value-based arrangement, Stimson went directly to employers, such as the Metro Nashville Public Schools. In its bundled arrangements, VUMC's actuarial team sets bundle prices using historical utilization rates and internal cost, charge, and revenue data. VUMC assumes financial risk and, as of mid-2024, is making margin and improving market share on service lines included in the MyHealth Bundles program.

As Stimson explained VUMC's motivation in a conversation with me: "The reason we are doing this is not simply to hit growth and financial targets. The mission is to deliver the best patient care experience. We want to leverage bundled payments so providers are free to do their best work and are rewarded for that effort. When you think in this way, the bundled payments really are just a tool, a means of aligning our people around a shared purpose."

"If we didn't have the bundles," he added, "we would find another payment model to achieve the same outcome."

## The Strategies' Payoffs in 2024

As Porter's model predicted, the Vanderbilt strategies were synergistic. Building strong teams around PCCs and CSCs enabled VUMC to reap the benefits of bundled payments. Compensation incentives motivated leaders to meet goals, thus enabling PCCs to grow.

The organization chart is now much more complex. Dyads and triads are everywhere. Networks stretch across departments and divisions. As Burt noted in the introduction to *Brokerage and Closure* (2005), trust becomes increasingly important as matrix structures weaken the authority of each reporting relationship, and the Vanderbilt experience is a testament to the amount of trust – thick and thin – it took to transform the institution's approach to patient care and reimbursement,

The goal of changes at VUMC over the past 15 years was not to weaken authority. Vanderbilt was responding to imperatives for change introduced from the outside – and responding to outside imperatives is not usually a strength of academic medical centers. It is reasonable to argue that VUMC has used a social capital strategy and that teamwork has become one of its major competitive differentiators.

# Chapter 7

# How to Be a Chief Officer for Social Capital

The primary argument of this book is that managers at every level should see themselves as chief officers (COs) for social capital for their part of the organization. They should study the intensity and discipline that their chief financial officers (CFOs) bring to the work of building financial capital and consider how they might adapt those approaches to the work of building trustworthiness, teamwork, and high reliability in their part of the organization. The ability to learn from others is itself an important currency of social capital; in that spirit, managers becoming more like CFOs when it comes to social capital can be a competitive advantage in the uncertain times that lie ahead.

What does it mean for you to be CO for social capital? As is true for the CFO, your work begins with understanding current performance. For the people in your part of the organization, what do you know about their engagement and their alignment? Do you have a culture in which people feel respected and included and trust their colleagues? How do your patients and your colleagues view the commitment to teamwork and safety?

Just as the CFO undertakes financial forecasting, you should consider how the challenges of building social capital are likely to evolve. How is medical progress creating pressure for teamwork, because state-of-the-science care will be even more complex next year? How are cost pressures going to increase the urgency to redesign care? How will demographic and societal trends affect hiring and retaining an engaged workforce?

Just as the CFO has a growth mindset for financial capital, you should have a growth mindset for social capital. The currencies relevant to building social capital are clear and measurable: trust, pride, respect, teamwork, psychological safety, high reliability. They are drivers of engagement and alignment – which make people want to stay in their organization and make them resilient – and of performance in general.

The processes for amassing those currencies are also clear and measurable – building connections, strengthening those connections, and using the social networks that result to disseminate the values and behavioral norms that lead to better care. The work is nuanced; for example, there are bonding connections within groups and bridging connections across groups. There is thick trust – with people you see all the time – and thin trust – with people you may never see at all.

The work is also endlessly interesting, and the return on investment for managers themselves takes many forms. As described in Chapter 1, social science research indicates that managers flourish professionally if they are better at building social capital. On a personal basis, this work also brings out their best; after all, the pathway to earning trust is being trustworthy.

Although organizations usually have just one CFO, I think they need managers to play the analogous role for social capital at every level of the organization. When I have presented this idea to CFOs, they all seem to love it. I don't think they are just being polite to me, because they have rarely demonstrated that inclination in the past. As one CFO said to me, "We know the limits of what money can do." He and other CFOs are looking to managers to build social capital, so their organizations can achieve goals that would otherwise be out of reach. They should go about this by establishing objectives, making plans, and monitoring progress – just as CFOs do.

## Establishing Objectives for Building Social Capital

As a CO for social capital, you need to define objectives and set goals. Ask yourself:

1. What are our values?
2. What are we trying to achieve?
3. What does success mean?
4. What are the behavioral norms we need to attain if we are going to be consistent with our values and accomplish our goals?

The first question has probably already been discussed and answered in the C-suite and promulgated through messaging within the organization and to the public. For example, Mayo Clinic's slogan, "The needs of the patient come first," has been so widely disseminated within the Mayo system that it came up in almost every conversation I had with Mayo staff. Cleveland Clinic's "Patients first" is terser and Brigham and Women's "Helping our patients and families get back to what matters most" is more expansive, but all three express the same sentiments: We value our patients. Massachusetts General Hospital takes a different approach with "Our Strength Is Yours," which plays on the hospital's reputation as a top medical research center. That message implies "We're a medical powerhouse and we're going to bring everything we have to taking care of you."

The answer to the second question, "What are we trying to achieve?," is many layered. If you are CO for social capital for nutrition services, it can mean getting patients their meals on time. If you are CO for social capital of an integrated practice unit, it can mean getting care teams from different specialties to work together seamlessly. If you are the CO for social capital for the organization, it can mean getting every employee engaged in their work and aligned with the organization's mission.

The third question, "What does success mean?," can be answered by conducting surveys that measure patient experience, employee engagement, and staff alignment with your organization's values and mission. Pulse surveys conducted at regular intervals over months give real-time snapshots of how you're doing. More detailed surveys measure improvement over quarters or years.

The fourth question, "How do we translate our values into behavioral norms?," is more challenging, but addressing it is a critical step in creating competitive differentiation through social capital. The first step is asking "What are the behaviors that should define what it means to be someone who works in our organization?" If your answer is "To be determined," the time to determine them is now.

You need organizational goals to determine behavioral ideals and to work toward making them behavioral norms. In the past, leaders might have advocated for behavioral norms that enhanced hospitality – like using people's names, making eye contact, picking up trash in the corridors. Those are all still desirable, but our times demand behavioral norms that go deeper in meeting the emotional needs of employees and patients – they want to feel safe; they want to know everyone is working together; they want to trust.

What would it take to achieve goals like Zero Harm, 100% trust, and respect that is as second nature as hand hygiene? It would take thinking like a CO for social capital, acting like a CO for social capital, and working like a CO for social capital.

## Thinking Like a CO for Social Capital

Nothing is more important than the frame of mind you bring to the work of building social capital. Your outlook influences how you form connections, lead teams, and use networks – and your outlook is likely to set the tone for your teams and networks. Research has identified two successful strategies that strengthen teams and networks throughout an organization – adopting a growth mindset and thinking like a coach.

## *Adopting a Growth Mindset*

Stanford psychologist Carol Dweck (2007) has proposed a simple but powerful approach that can guide your decisions and interactions – adopting a growth mindset. As Dweck explains, people who believe their talents can be developed – through hard work, good strategies, and input from others – have a growth mindset. People with a growth mindset are more likely to move out of their comfort zones because they expect to learn something in the process. If they don't meet their goals, they keep trying because they believe they can eventually get there.

In contrast, people with a fixed mindset believe their talents are innate. They attribute their successes to their native intelligence and tend to see failures as evidence of their limitations and lack of potential.

People with a growth mindset get more done because they worry less about looking smart and put more energy into learning. When entire companies embrace a growth mindset, their employees report feeling far more empowered and committed; employees also receive greater organizational support for collaboration and innovation (Dweck, 2016).

A team or organization with a growth mindset has implicit respect for its members. By assuming the attitude "we have the ability to learn and improve and accomplish our goals," leaders are conveying that they value and trust employees. They are also creating a safe environment because setbacks are not met with blame and recrimination but viewed as learning opportunities.

## Thinking Like a Coach

To build great teams, COs for social capital need more than being told to create teamwork. To apply a well-known framework from Simon Sinek, who runs the Golden Circle website (https://simonsinek.com/golden-circle), managers need to understand:

- *Why* they are asking the people reporting to them to work together more effectively. In other words, front-line managers should understand and embrace the organizational goals like Zero Harm, reducing patients' suffering, and making healthcare affordable.

- *How* they can build social capital through teamwork. Managers should understand that a critical part of their role is fostering and strengthening connections among the people reporting to them and spreading the right norms and values across those connections.

- *What* key steps they can take to build social capital. For example, managers should create a playbook for strengthening their connections to members of their teams, such as rounding on two of them every shift – and not just the two who are the most enjoyable to interact with. There should be regular meetings of the team to review data and progress toward their goals.

In other words, COs for social capital need to think like coaches. Good coaches know how to be role models for their teams. They respect every teammate. They keep their focus on the goal. They share responsibility for the outcome. They decide what to expect of the team and communicate their expectations clearly.

I learned the value of clear communication when I started getting involved in quality improvement at my hospital. My father told me that there were many good books on management, but he was only going to give me one. It was a thin paperback called *Language in Thought in Action*, by S. I. Hayakawa (1941), the former U.S. Senator and linguistics professor. "It will help you learn to get precise about language," my father said.

"Management is harder than it looks," he added. "It will be a big help if communication is clear. If someone says they will be there in a few minutes, it might mean 180 seconds to one person and a half hour to the person who said it. When the same words mean different things to different people, it's a problem. Try to get your colleagues to be clear in how they communicate, and you should be clear yourself."

It was good advice. This recommendation is consistent with the first steps taken to reduce safety events across Community Health Services (CHS), the 71-hospital system. One of those initial steps was to standardize the nomenclature used across the organization for safety events along with how data were collected and analyzed. The description of "Zero Harm" in the CHS case study in Chapter 4 is another example of standardizing language.

For managers working in organizations of any size, the work to standardize language can be annoying and difficult. However, it is impossible to drive improvement in diversity, equity, and inclusion, for example, unless everyone collects demographic data the same way. It is difficult to drive improvement in teamwork unless everyone measures it the same way and has access to benchmark data based on the same methods. And it is hard to know when to expect someone to show up unless everyone avoids vague language like "in a few minutes."

Unfortunately, few of us are born great communicators or superb coaches. But with a growth mindset and a little coaching, we can become very good at both.

A program undertaken by the Medical University of South Carolina (MUSC) in Charleston illustrates how much a coaching program can accomplish. The program focused on work units with low employee engagement (Tier 3 in its categorization based on employee surveys), low culture of safety (below 25th percentile according to national benchmarks), or low patient experience (below the median according to national benchmarks).

The implementation of the program was no-nonsense in tone. The leaders of these units attended a kick-off meeting hosted by their divisional chief executive officers (CEOs), where their need to participate in the program was conveyed. Unit leaders signed a participation agreement, which was cosigned by their supervisor. Coaches were chosen from staff working on employee engagement, patient safety, and patient experience teams and were asked to complete a coaching program through the International Coaching Federation. Throughout the following year, the coaches monitored the actual participation by the unit leaders and gave reports to the leaders' supervisors; leaders who did not participate were not allowed to stay in their roles.

The coaches were trained to analyze data in their areas of focus and in skills like team building, conflict resolution, and communicating clearly. The results were encouraging, with measurable improvements in employee engagement, the culture of safety, and patient experience.

For employee engagement, 78% of the low-engagement units had risen out of that category. For safety culture, the success rate was 94%. And for patient experience, the success rate was 95%. These unit-level improvements contributed to overall improvements at MUSC from 2022 to 2024 in employee engagement (from 4.02 to 4.09 using Press Ganey's 5-point scales), culture of safety (3.94–4.05), and patients' overall likelihood of recommending MUSC (Scheurer et al. 2025).

At the end of their training, participants were thinking like coaches and acting like COs for social capital.

# Acting Like a CO for Social Capital

The most important role of a CO for social capital at any level is to translate the organization's values into behavioral norms. Organization executives and frontline managers have different tools to accomplish this: executives can inculcate norms organization-wide; frontline managers can do so through the teams and networks they have built. Both functions are important and essential.

## *Acting Like a CO for Social Capital at the Top*

Organization leaders are always on display – or at least they should be. They can win or lose the loyalty of their employees based on what they pay attention to, how they recruit talent and say good-bye to those leaving the organization, the stories that they tell, and how they respond to crises.

To act like a CO for social capital is to encourage the behaviors you want to see become organizational norms – behaviors like respect, trustworthiness, and inclusion. Translating values into behaviors is rarely simple or easy. The willingness to define behavioral norms and then enforce them can cause discomfort in the conflict-averse culture of healthcare, but it is an essential step in building social capital. Leaders at several organizations have ensured that all employees are aware of behavioral norms by strategically posting them throughout the organization.

At Vanderbilt University Medical Center (VUMC), for example, all caregivers are aware of the organization's credo, which is based on six major points:

1. I make those I serve my highest priority.
2. I respect privacy and confidentiality.
3. I communicate effectively.
4. I conduct myself professionally.
5. I have a sense of ownership.
6. I am committed to my colleagues. (Vanderbilt University Medical Center 2024)

But where the credo really comes to life are the bullet points under each of these major points. For example, beneath "I make those I serve my highest priority" are commitments including:

- Promote the health and well-being of all patients who seek care at Vanderbilt.
- Respect colleagues and those we serve who differ by gender, race, religion, culture, national origin, mental and physical abilities, and sexual orientation and treat them with dignity, respect and compassion.
- Recognize that every member of the Vanderbilt team makes important contributions.
- Ensure that all team members understand overall team goals and their roles.
- Answer questions posed by patients, trainees, or staff to ensure understanding and facilitate learning. (Vanderbilt University Medical Center 2024)

When someone is behaving in ways that are not consistent with the credo, people will say "That's not credo" to others and sometimes directly to the offender. The subtitles on posters with the credo say "It's who we are," and while not everyone at VUMC adheres to the credo 100% of the time, it is a set of behaviors that helps define what it means to be part of the group.

Expressing behavioral norms in detail right in the place where they are relevant is important. At Oklahoma University's delivery system, OU Health, for example, signs are posted in conference rooms that list 10 "Behavioral Ground Rules." There probably are no areas in healthcare where these ground rules would not improve decision making, and posting them is a useful way of turning them into norms.

1. The patient always has a voice in the room.
2. Robustly debate in the room with civility and leave with one voice.
3. Hold ourselves and each other accountable.
4. Provide and invite direct, constructive feedback.
5. Be the expert and respect others' expertise.
6. Own the whole before your piece.
7. Lead by example with a voice of optimism and hope.
8. Decision making is data-driven and decisive.
9. Advocate and support colleagues – act as one team.
10. Be fully present and prepared.

Another expression of norms that acknowledges the value of reciprocity is the Physician Compact developed at Virginia Mason Medical Center, which has now been adapted at many other organizations (American Hospital Association 2024). The compact has two columns – one is the physician's responsibilities to the organization, and the other is the organization's responsibilities to physicians.

Among the items included among physician's responsibilities is a mandate to collaborate on care delivery:

- Include staff, physicians, and management on team.
- Treat all members with respect.
- Demonstrate the highest levels of ethnical and professional conduct.
- Behave in a manner consistent with group goals.

Included in the organization's responsibilities are:

- Provide information and tools necessary to improve practice.
- Create an environment that supports teams and individuals.
- Manage and lead organization with integrity and accountability.

Having created norms, organizations must have enforcement mechanisms so that the norms have meaning and can influence outcomes. University of North Carolina (UNC) Health (2024) identified clear behaviors and practices called "Carolina Care," which are incorporated into its stated values. For organizations to have a formal affiliation or integration with UNC Health, they must adopt Carolina Care standards.

For C-suite managers, creating a genuine connection with every employee, though a lovely idea, is often a physical impossibility. However, managers still can demonstrate that they embrace the organization's values by making and explaining decisions that support them. They can convey trustworthiness by following through on commitments – whether to increase diversity and inclusion at all levels or to expand free shuttle service for employees. They can show reciprocity by inviting – and actively considering – input from all levels of the organization and from patients as well. They can communicate caring and authenticity by being on call in times of crisis.

They can also employ internal marketing to help get the message across. Some may cringe at that last suggestion because they think of marketing as smoke and mirrors that obscure the absence of substance. Yet marketing campaigns can sharpen the organization's brand, which can help leaders reliably live up to the aspirational identity. They can even initiate cultural transformations.

One of my favorite examples of a transformative marketing initiative is Cleveland Clinic's "Patients First" campaign, whose chief advocate was Toby Cosgrove, CEO from 2004 to 2017. Cosgrove might have seemed an unlikely candidate to put empathy for patients at the core of the Cleveland Clinic's self-image. He had emerged as a leader based on his extraordinary record as a cardiac surgeon. To Cleveland

Clinic employees, he embodied traditional healthcare physician leadership – awe-inspiring and intimidating.

But Cosgrove realized that leading the Cleveland Clinic required something beyond the skills that made him a successful surgeon. As he told me, "I realized that people respected us, but they didn't like us very much." Patients would come to the Cleveland Clinic to have surgery to fix problems like leaking heart valves, but they didn't always leave feeling cared for. He concluded that that had to change.

The message Cosgrove gave in his first major address as CEO of the organization was that the Cleveland Clinic had to put patients first. He said that without patients, there would be no reason for the clinic to exist. Doctors, nurses, and other employees were important, of course, but the needs and the experiences of patients had to be the clear top priority. It wasn't rhetoric; he was articulating a culture change that he intended to lead (Cleveland Clinic 2017). To make that point, he had lapel buttons saying "Patients First" distributed to every employee at his speech and then throughout the organization.

I asked him whether he thought his colleagues were going to roll their eyes when he decided to give out those buttons, and he told me, "Yes. I decided that I was going to pretend I didn't see them and push right on ahead."

The lapel buttons were just the beginning of the work. Soon thereafter, his team created the Cleveland Clinic empathy video (2013), which went viral internationally, helping caregivers recognize that empathy was core to their self-identity. What may have seemed like a public relations flourish led to employee alignment with the hospital's mission; it's impossible to visit the Cleveland Clinic today without running into someone wearing a "Patients First" button.

## Acting Like a CO for Social Capital on the Front Line

Frontline managers have countless opportunities to reinforce behavioral norms – through rounding, huddles, structured meetings, and casual encounters. They are acting like COs for social capital by making an effort to get to know their team members, creating an atmosphere of safety and respect, acknowledging their successes, and offering constructive feedback when they fall short.

Organizational behaviorists Ginka Toegel and Jean-Louis Barsoux (2024) suggest that managers perform a short self-audit at the end of each week by answering three questions for each of their direct reports:

1. Did you seek the person's company?
2. Did you acknowledge the person's capabilities?
3. Did you assist the person's growth? (p. 149)

Answering "no" to any question for any employee for two or three weeks in a row is a signal to search deeper for connections, such as shared interests, or to solicit those employees, input more frequently. Managers who have persistent difficulty connecting with team members should seek training or coaching support.

Tracking and supporting the improvement of front-line managers is critical for building social capital. Take nurse managers, for example. Being a nurse manager requires more than being an excellent caregiver; it necessitates managing staffing levels, budgeting, allocating resources appropriately, mentoring staff, and fostering a culture of continuous learning. And how well nurse managers do their jobs has a big influence on whether the nursing staff are content and motivated or ready to quit. Yet many nurses are promoted to managers without training in any of those areas.

My colleagues have analyzed the impact of nurse managers' performance using data from the National Database of Nursing Quality Indicators. Across all clinical settings, units with top-quartile nurse managers had 21 to 32% more nurses reporting an intent to stay compared with units with nurse managers in the bottom quartile. The units with top-performing nurse managers also have better nurse-reported quality of care, fewer falls, fewer central line–associated bloodstream infections, fewer catheter-associated urinary tract infections, and better patient experience (Warshawsky 2023).

The nursing data lead to a commonsense conclusion that is applicable to all settings in healthcare organizations: Frontline managers should be supported with training and understand their accountability for creating a genuine con-nection with every person reporting to them (Toegel and Barsoux 2024).

## Acting as CO for Social Capital at Any Level by Using Digital Technology

The availability of text messaging, email, video meetings, and patient portals has transformed communications within organizations and between caregivers and patients. When used strategically, they can build social capital almost overnight, as the Cleveland Clinic learned when its empathy video went viral.

While digital communication had been a good-to-have tool since the turn of the century, COVID-19 pandemic made it a must-have capability. With in-person gatherings on hold indefinitely, top leadership had an opportunity to build social capital by quickly adopting digital technologies like email, text messaging, and Zoom to hold frequent meetings and town halls in which they could relay updates on their hospitals' status, pass along the latest evidence-based information on the spread of the virus, and address fears about layoffs. There was another advantage to using digital communication: When CEOs talked to employees from their homes, it made them seem more human and the connection more intimate.

These new technologies have the potential to strengthen connections between employees and their organizations by improving the ability of leaders to listen and be visible as they do so. An interesting new approach for strengthening connections is "gamification." A social gaming app developed by Charge Health, a Press Ganey partner, allows caregivers to show support and recognition for each other. Employees respond to queries like "Who is the first person you ask when you have a tough question?" and "Who is most likely to win a quality award?" Positive messages are sent to nurses identified through the polls. In early experience with this app, the number of users grew to 20% of the total nursing workforce during the first four weeks, and metrics like daily average-use rates were high for a social gaming app (Guney and Robertson 2024).

Digital technologies strengthen connections between the organization and employees because they serve as improved versions of the bygone suggestion box. Crowdsourcing, as Case Study 7.1 demonstrates, is valuable not just for the new knowledge created but also because employees like being asked what they think. When leaders act in response to the information they gain, they prove that they are truly interested in what employees have to say.

---

**Case Study 7.1  Eastern Carolina University Health: Using Crowdsourcing to Build a Culture of Respect**

In 2021, Eastern Carolina University (ECU) Health decided to start a "system-wide effort to foster a culture of respect (Thompson et al., 2024)." Like most other healthcare organizations, this 1,447-bed health system in eastern North Carolina had confronted morale and workforce retention challenges as the COVID pandemic unfolded. Employee engagement data showed that a strong driver required system attention: results related to perceptions of respect from the organization, as well as employees' perceptions of respect from and

---

for supervisors. ECU's Office of Experience decided to begin with a study "to understand how [employees] defined respect, to document lived experience, and to determine how respect could be restored when broken or preserved."

ECU Health did not want to replicate what so many organizations had done – form a committee with nebulous goals, no authority to change anything, and no delivery date. Instead, it used the five-stage design thinking process – empathize, define, ideate, prototype, and test – to address what it considered a "wicked problem": lack of respect in the workplace. It started a four-week idea campaign, using a crowdsourcing platform (provided by my colleagues at Press Ganey) to get feedback and activation from as much of the workforce as possible. There was a two-week "ideation phase" and then a two-week voting phase, followed by design work to integrate the top-priority initiatives into life at ECU.

In the ideation phase, team members from all ECU Health entities were asked to address three issues:

1. Define respect in their own terms.

2. Name one practice the organization should stop.

3. Provide ideas and suggestions for creating a culture of respect.

Responses to these questions led to development of 33 ideas, with common themes identified in Table 7.1.

*(continued)*

*How to Be a Chief Officer for Social Capital*

**Table 7.1** Common themes identified in responses to the questions about respect.

**Phase 1 Questions and common themes from ECU respect initiative**

| Questions | What does respect mean to you? | Name one thing we should stop doing. | What suggestions do you have to create a culture of respect in the organization? Name one thing we should start doing. |
|---|---|---|---|
| Common themes: | • Acknowledgment of all team members, their contributions<br>• Valuing time<br>• Focus on personal interactions | • Showing favoritism<br>• Promoting competition<br>• Forgetting to follow up on commitments<br>• Interpersonal communication (surveys vs. conversations) | • Encouraging safe space for communication (roundtables, focus groups, and discussions)<br>• Shadowing to gain a respect for the work of others<br>• Making regular reminders to show respect<br>• Producing video examples depicting respect in the workplace |

*Source:* Thompson et al., 2024. Reprinted with permission, *NEJM Catalyst* (catalyst.nejm.org) ©Massachusetts Medical Society.

After the 33 specific ideas with these themes were generated, ECU employees were invited to vote on the ideas and comments that "resonated most with them."

The crowdsourcing technology used sophisticated methods to develop the rankings. As described by ECU's team:

Voters were prompted to select one of two ideas presented on the screen at one time. After each selection, a different pairing would appear, allowing them to select their preference from each pair presented. Voters never saw the same pair twice. This PairMatrix voting system was designed by the vendor to prevent individuals or groups from manipulating results to favor specific ideas. Instead, data emerged only after each voter was presented with multiple pairs of ideas, ensuring unbiased data.

The work of crowdsourcing may seem labor-intensive or time-intensive to the uninitiated, but it need not be. As ECU authors described, "One team member devoted approximately eight hours per week to manage the tool. This included time to design the content and to monitor/report results. Everything else was automated or developed by the vendor" – my colleagues at Press Ganey. Table 7.2 shows the top 10 ideas as ranked by the 2,353 employees who participated in the crowdsourcing.

The next phase was led by ECU's internal "experience design" team, headed by an internal expert trained in design research. The design team led multiple

*(continued)*

*How to Be a Chief Officer for Social Capital*

**Table 7.2** Top 10 ideas revealed in popular voting.

| Rank | Votes | Summary |
| --- | --- | --- |
| 1 | 76% | Understand each team member's contributions to the organization. |
| 2 | 75% | Promote acknowledgment and meaningful encounters. |
| 3 | 72% | Support a life-work balance and time off. |
| 4 | 70% | Honor others based on their actions and character. |
| 5 | 66% | Respect the time of others and honor commitments. |
| 6 | 64% | Provide safe space for a person's authentic self to be present, asking, listening and acting with positive intent and constructive feedback. |
| 7 | 63% | Honor loyalty to the organization. |
| 8 | 61% | Consider and support a person's feelings, rights, wishes, or experiences. |
| 9 | 61% | Respect a team member's space and time to disconnect after hours. |
| 10 | 56% | Believe in and acknowledge intrinsic worth, dignity and regard for another. Model respectful behaviors. |

*Source*: Thompson et al., 2024 © Massachusetts Medical Society. Reprinted with permission, NEJM Catalyst (catalyst.nejm.org) © Massachusetts Medical Society.

*Social Capital in Healthcare*

three-hour interactive sessions at three hospitals to explore how to apply the top 10 ideas. Table 7.3 shows the major themes and ideas that developed.

In their description of the conclusions from this phase, ECU leaders wrote:

Team members explained that one's sense of belonging on the care team could be significantly impacted by the level of respect displayed by those of influence and authority on the team. Some researchers have implied an even greater impact. Hershcovis and colleagues [2017] argue that belonging is impacted by respectful behavior of anyone on the team, regardless of their position of power. Team members suggested leaders should set an expectation for respectful behavior.

After the design work, one-hour interactive sessions entitled "Fostering a Culture of Respect" were conducted at all nine hospitals in the system. The discussions that followed at each institution led to adopting specific steps chosen locally. At two hospitals, for example, "respect kits" were developed to promote communication about how employees wished to be treated. The kits include stickers that employees can wear to convey emotional needs to their colleagues (e.g., "Desire encouragement" or "Need quiet space to think"). The overall organization developed an "ECU Health Respect in the Workplace" video.

Has the program worked? Responses to the statement "This hospital treats team members with respect" improved by 0.07 compared to before the program, but

*(continued)*

*How to Be a Chief Officer for Social Capital*

**Table 7.3** Design intent and proposed solution to foster a culture of respect.

| *Intent* | **Ideas** |
| --- | --- |
| Inspire Respect through Empathy | Create a shadowing program for all team members to learn about the value of diverse roles in the organization. |
| See the Person | Encourage managers to learn about what matters to individuals on their team.<br>Invite team members to share more about how they prefer to be treated, how they prefer to work, and what matters to them. |
| Honoring Feelings and Individual Preferences | Develop icons that represent diverse feelings and invite team members to wear a sticker or button to help others understand how they wish to be treated. |
| Acknowledgment | Host events to acknowledge team members for their contributions and respectful behavior. |
| Shared Decision-making | Engage in open conversation that encourages and utilizes feedback from team members. |

*Source*: Thompson et al., 2024 © Massachusetts Medical Society. Reprinted with permission, *NEJM Catalyst* (catalyst.nejm.org) © Massachusetts Medical Society.

another important finding related to social capital is also clear – asking employees what they think is a good thing to do. ECU Health soon started other crowdsourcing challenges on issues such as how to reduce waste. By mid-2024, its most recent crowdsourcing event (on new behavioral standards) had over 6,000 employees casting more than 73,000 votes.

Did the employees of ECU roll their eyes at the opportunity posed by being asked what they thought? The opposite seems to be true. While the national average for employee engagement declined from 2021 to 2023, ECU Health's rose from the 18th to the 33rd percentile. And ECU Health exceeded the national average on the item "I am involved in the decisions that affect my work."

# Building Social Capital by Instilling Hope

In 2013, I wrote a piece called "The Word That Shall Not Be Spoken" in *The New England Journal of Medicine* (Lee 2013), which got a lot of attention, including a front-page story in *the New York Times* (Kolata 2015, p. 1). The article was about how many people working in medicine and writing about it (including those at *The New England Journal* itself) were uncomfortable with the word "suffering." The most obvious explanation was that it made us feel guilty. We knew suffering existed, but, as one colleague put it, "If I thought my job was reducing suffering, I'd never get home at night."

In the years since, things have changed. Perhaps it is partly because awareness of suffering spreads so readily via social media now. In any case, the reduction of suffering *is* widely accepted as our job now, and our understanding of the ways in which people suffer has become more nuanced. Suffering includes feeling disrespect. It includes feeling buffeted by systems that do not seem to care whether you are confused or anxious or caught in some irrational Catch-22 loop. It includes feeling unsafe, even if you are not unsafe.

But strong connections between patients and their caregivers are not just for painful information. That is why I want to end this book with a positive way to use connections with patients – giving hope as a high reliability function.

Experienced clinicians often have the same response when patients say they feel hopeless. "There's always hope," they say. "The question is, what are we hoping for?" Sometimes the hope is for a cure. Sometimes it is for arresting disease progression. Sometimes it is for as much good time as possible. And sometimes it is for a relief of suffering and a death with dignity.

Hoping should be a social function. Clinicians and patients need to discuss what it is reasonable to hope for, and what they can do to maximize the chances of reaching it – together. Patients should know that they are not alone in their hopes – that their clinicians share their hopes with them and are their partners in trying to realize them.

My colleague Deirdre Mylod and I drew on survey and comment data from patients and described a "Hope Framework Checklist" aimed at helping clinicians give hope with high reliability (Mylod and Lee 2023). It includes advice to clinicians like:

- Be direct in asking patients what they currently hope for.
- Probe both what is desired and what is dreaded.
- Share realistic feedback in a supportive way, describing what *can* be accomplished.
- Discuss and prioritize actions to maximize wellness and minimize burden of condition.
- Convey intention to help and commitment to the patient's journey.
- Communicate prior experience with patients on a similar journey.
- Describe how and when you will together evaluate the progress being made or alternatives to be explored.

As we wrote in the article:

> This checklist requires physicians to think through with patients what is probable, what is possible and what steps might close the gap. And it also requires clinicians to have conversations with patients and families with the specific intent of creating shared understanding. Giving hope is successful when all parties share the same hopes and adjust their hopes together (Mylod and Lee 2023).

My hope is that this book has made that case that every manager really can function like a CO for social capital, and if they do, it will be good for their organizations, their patients, and themselves. I include physicians and other clinicians in the category of "managers" since they directly oversee and influence the care of patients. I hope that I have made the argument that building social capital is important for responding to changes in healthcare and that it has strategic importance for healthcare organizations.

In an era when financial capital and human capital have so many constraints, the ability of organizations to build social capital arguably represents the most important approach to achieving advantage – where "advantage" means positive differentiation from competitors. As I observed earlier in this chapter, every CFO has a growth mindset when it comes to financial capital – and every manager should have a growth mindset when it comes to social capital.

# References

Agency for Healthcare Research and Quality. 2019, September 7. "High reliability." *Patient Safety Net.* https://psnet.ahrq.gov/primer/high-reliability

American Hospital Association. 2024. "Physician Compact." https://trustees.aha.org/physician-compact.

Bates, David W., David M. Levine, Hojjat Salmasian et al. 2023. "The safety of inpatient health care." *New England Journal of Medicine* 388 (2): 142–153.

Beach, Mary Catherine. 2024. "Disrespect in health care: An epistemic injustice. *Journal of Health Services Research & Policy* 29 (1): 1–2. https://doi.org/10.1177/13558196231212851

Beckerman, Jacqueline. 2024, January 30. "Diversifying the patient-family advisory council." *NEJM Catalyst.* https://catalyst.nejm.org/doi/full/10.1056/CAT.24.0039

Bourdieu, Pierre. 1986. "The forms of capital." In: *Handbook of Theory and Research for the Sociology of Education* (ed. J. Richardson), 241–258. Westport, CT: Greenwood Press.

Burt, Ronald S. 2005. *Brokerage & Closure: An Introduction to Social Capital.* Oxford, UK: Oxford University Press.

Carlson, Brian, Richelle Graham, Brad Stinson, and Jordan LaRocca. 2022. "Teamwork that affects outcomes: A method to enhance team ownership. *Patient Experience Journal* 9 (2): 94–98.

Christakis, Nicholas A. and James H. Fowler. 2007. "The spread of obesity in a large social network over 32 years. *New England Journal of Medicine* 357 (4): 370–379.

Christakis, Nicholas A. and James H. Fowler. 2009. *Connected: The Surprising Power of Our Social Networks and How They Shape Our Lives—How*

*Your Friends' Friends' Friends Affect Everything You Feel, Think, and Do*. New York: Little, Brown Spark.

Cleveland Clinic. 2017, December 27. "New Cleveland Clinic CEO can count on 51,000 caregivers for smooth transition. https://newsroom .clevelandclinic.org/2017/12/27/new-cleveland-clinic-ceo-can-count -on-51000-caregivers-for-smooth-transition

Cleveland Clinic. 2013. "Empathy: The Human Connection to Patient Care." https://www.youtube.com/watch?v=cDDWvj_q-o8

Cooperrider, David L., and Suresh Srivastva. 1987. "Appreciative inquiry in organizational life." In: *Research in Organizational Change and Development*, vol. 1 (ed. R.W. Woodman and W.A. Pasmore), 129–169. Stamford, CT: JAI Press.

Darzi, Ara, and Thomas H. Lee. 2020, August 19. "Lessons from the London Stroke Initiative: How Pathway Improvement Is discovered, designed, and deployed." *NEJM Catalyst.* https://catalyst.nejm.org/doi/ full/10.1056/CAT.20.0470

Definitive Healthcare. 2023, November 16. "Average age of doctors and providers by medical specialty." *Nurse Leader.* https://www.nurseleader .com/action/showPdf?pii=S1541-4612%2821%2900054-9/

Dempsey, Christina. 2021, June. "The impact of compassionate, connected care on safety, quality, and experience in the age of Covid-19." *Nurse Leader.* https://www.nurseleader.com/article/S1541-4612(21)00054-9/fulltext

Dudley, Jessica, Sarah McLaughlin, and Thomas H. Lee. 2022, January 19. "Why so many women physicians are quitting." *Harvard Business Review.* https://hbr.org/2022/01/why-so-many-women-physicians-are-quitting

Dunbar, Robin. 2021. *Friends: Understanding the Power of Our Most Important Relationships*. London: Little Brown.

Dweck, Carol S. 2007. *"Mindset." The New Psychology of Success*. New York: Ballantine Books.

Dweck, Carol. 2016, January 13. "What having a 'growth mindset' actually means." *Harvard Business Review.* https://hbr.org/2016/01/what-having-a-growth-mindset-actually-means

Edmondson, Amy C. 2012. *Teaming: How Organizations Learn, Innovate, and Compete in the Knowledge Economy*. San Francisco: Wiley.

Ericsson, K. Anders, Michael J. Prietula, and Edward T, Cokely, 2007. "'The making of an expert." *Harvard Business Review.* https://hbr .org/2007/07/the-making-of-an-expert. https://www.nurseleader.com/ article/S1541-4612(21)00054-9/fulltext

Feldman, Jonah, Katherine A. Hochman, Benedict Vincent Guzman et al. 2024. "Scaling note quality assessment across an academic medical center with AI and GPT-4.". *NEJM Catalyst* 5 (5): https://doi.org/10.1056/ CAT.23.0283

Fogg, Jane F., and Christine A. Sinsky.. 2023. "In-basket reduction: A multiyear pragmatic approach to lessen the work burden of primary care physicians." *NEJM Catalyst* 4 (5): http://doi.org/10.1056/CAT.22.0438

Frei, Frances X., and Anne Morriss. 2020, May–June. "Begin with trust." *Harvard Business Review.* https://hbr.org/2020/05/begin-with-trust

Gallo, Amy. 2023, February 15. "What is psychological safety?" *Harvard Business Review.* https://hbr.org/2023/02/what-is-psychological-safety

Gandhi, Tejal K., Derek Feeley, and Dan Schummers. 2020. "Zero harm in health care." *NEJM Catalyst* 1 (2): https://catalyst.nejm.org/doi/ abs/10.1056/CAT.19.1137

Goralnick, Eric, and Jonathan Gates. 2013. "We fight like we train." *New England Journal of Medicine* 368 (21): 1960–1961.

Guney, Senem, and Kyle Robertson. 2024. "More than a game: Building a workplace culture of positivity and belonging among nurses." *Journal of Nursing Administration* 54 (6): 327–332.

Guney, Senem, Zach Childers, and Thomas H. Lee. 2021, April 2. "Understanding unhappy patients makes hospitals better for everyone." *Harvard Business Review.* https://hbr.org/2021/04/understanding-unhappy-patients-makes-hospitals-better-for-everyone

Hargrave, Marshall. 2024, July 11. "Capital: Definition, how it's used, structure, and types in business." Investopedia. https://www.investopedia .com/terms/c/capital.asp

Harrison, Marc. 2018, March 7. "Tiered escalation huddles yield rapid results." *NEJM Catalyst.* https://catalyst.nejm.org/doi/abs/10.1056/CAT.18.0239

Hayakawa, S.I. 1941. *Language in Thought and Action.* New York: Houghton Mifflin Harcourt.

Hershcovis, M. Sandy, Babatunde Ogunfowora, Tara C. Reich, and Amy M. Christie. 2017. "Targeted workplace incivility: The roles of belongingness, embarrassment, and power." *Journal of Organizational Behavior* 38 (7): 1057–1075.

Jones, Jeffrey M. 2021, March 29. "U.S. church membership falls below majority for first time." Gallup. https://news.gallup.com/poll/341963/church-membership-falls-below-majority-first-time.aspx

Joshi, Maulik. 2022, March 9. "Just huddle." *NEJM Catalyst*. https://catalyst.nejm.org/doi/full/10.1056/CAT.22.0007

Kelleher, Stacey. 2024, February 29. "The demand on female physicians: What's at atake?" *Health eCareers*. https://www.healthecareers.com/career-resources/industry-news/staff-and-patients-ask-more-of-female-primary-care-physicians

Kolata, Gina. 2015, February 17. "Doctors strive to do less harm by inattentive care." *New York Times*. https://www.nytimes.com/2015/02/18/health/doctors-strive-to-do-less-harm-by-inattentive-care.html?hp&action=click&pgtype=Homepage&module=photo-spot-region&region=top-news&WT.nav=top-news&_r=0

Lee, Thomas H, 2005. "Quiet in the library." *New England Journal of Medicine* 352 (11): 1068.

Lee, Thomas H. 2013. "The word that shall not be spoken." *New England Journal of Medicine* 369 (19): 1777–1779.

Lee, Thomas H. 2016. *An Epidemic of Empathy in Healthcare*. New York: McGraw Hill.

Lee, Thomas H. 2021. "Zoom family meeting." *New England Journal of Medicine* 384 (17): 1586–1587.

Lee, Thomas H., and Nell Buhlman. 2024, August 9. "The strongest U.S. healthcare organizations invest in social capital." *Harvard Business Review*. https://hbr.org/2024/08/the-strongest-u-s-healthcare-organizations-invest-in-social-capital

Lee, Thomas H., Senem Guney, and Deirdre E. Mylod. 2023. "What patient-experience data reveal about trust." *Hastings Center Report* 53 (Suppl. 2): S46–S52. https://doi.org/10.1002/hast.1523

Levine, David M., Ania Syrowatka, Hojjat Salmasian et al. 2024. "The safety of outpatient health care: Review of electronic health records." *Annals of Internal Medicine* 177 (6): 738–748.

Mather, Mark, and Paola Scommegna. 2024, January 9. "Fact sheet: Aging in the United States." *Population Reference Bureau.* https://www.prb.org/resources/fact-sheet-aging-in-the-united-states

McChrystal, Stanley, Tantum Collins, David Silverman, and Chris Fussell. 2015. *Team of Teams: New Rules of Engagement for a Complex World.* New York: Portfolio/Penguin.

McCluskey, Priyanka Dayal. 2016, June 27. "At Brigham, a day of relief tinged with bitterness." *Boston Globe.* https://www.bostonglobe.com/business/2016/06/27/brigham-officials-nurses-express-relief-preempting-strike/ffIruPmLtY8t83umkKGRHJ/story.html

Murthy, Vivek H. 2023. *Our Epidemic of Loneliness and Isolation. The U.S. Surgeon General's Advisory on the Healing Effects of Social Connection and Community.* https://www.hhs.gov/sites/default/files/surgeon-general-social-connection-advisory.pdf

Mylod, Deirdre and Thomas H. Lee. 2023. "Giving hope as a high reliability function of healthcare." *Journal of Patient Experience* 10: https://www.nychealthandhospitals.org/pressrelease/20-new-wellness-rooms-open-to-support-healthcare-workers-well-being/

Obermeyer, Ziad, and Thomas H. Lee. 2017. "Lost in thought—the limits of the human mind and the future of medicine." *New England Journal of Medicine* 377 (13): 1209–1211.

Porter, Michael E. 2008, January. "The five competitive forces that shape strategy." *Harvard Business Review.* https://hbr.org/2008/01/the-five-competitive-forces-that-shape-strategy

Porter, Michael E. and Thomas H. Lee. 2013. "The strategy that will fix health care." *Harvard Business Review* 91: 50–70.

Porter, Michael E, and Thomas H. Lee. 2015. "Why strategy matters now." *New England Journal of Medicine* 372 (18): 1681–1684.

Porter, Michael E., and Thomas H. Lee. 2021, January 1. "Integrated practice units: A playbook for health care leaders." *NEJM Catalyst* 2. https://catalyst.nejm.org/doi/abs/10.1056/CAT.20.0237

Porter, Michael E, and Elizebeth O. Teisberg. 2006. *Redefining Health Care. Creating Value-Based Competition on Results*. Boston: Harvard Business School Press.

Putnam, Robert D. 2001. *Bowling Alone: The Collapse and Revival of American Community*. New York: Simon & Schuster.

Putnam, Robert D. 2020. *The Upswing: How Americans Came Together a Century Ago and How We Can Do It Again*. New York: Simon & Schuster.

Saltzman, Jonathan, and Andrea Estes. 2017, July 15. "At a four-star veterans' hospital: Care gets worse and worse." *Boston Globe*. https://www.bostonglobe.com/metro/2017/07/15/four-star-case-failure-manchester/n9VV7BerswvkL5akCgNzvK/story.html?event=event12

Scheurer, Danielle, Allen Coulter, Kristine Harper,, and Catherine Flanagan. 2025 (in press). "Coaching program to improve employee engagement, culture of safety, and patient experience." *NEJM Catalyst*.

Simon, Lynn T. and Terrie Van Buren. 2023. "Community health systems' ongoing journey to zero preventable harm." *NEJM Catalyst* 4 (12): https://catalyst.nejm.org/doi/full/10.1056/CAT.23.0250

Skinner, Lucy, Max Yates, David I. Auerbach, Peter I. Buerhaus, and Douglas O. Staiger. 2023. "Marriage, children, and sex-based differences in physician hours and income." *JAMA Health Forum* 4 (3): https://jamanetwork.com/journals/jama-health-forum/fullarticle/2802875

Smith, Timothy M. 2023, July 31. "Generational trends underlie doctors' move from private practice." AMA. https://www.ama-assn.org/practice-management/private-practices/generational-trends-underlie-doctors-move-private-practice

Thompson, Tammy, Christina Bowen, Julie Oehlert, Katrissa Fisher, and Boya Zhang. 2024. "Codesigning Solutions with health care team members to foster a culture of respect." *NEJM Catalyst* 5, no. 11. https://catalyst.nejm.org/stoken/default+domain/CB3DNS9EEZN3WPWRFYBU/full?redirectUri=/doi/full/10.1056/CAT.23.020

Toegel, Ginka, and Jean-Louis Barsoux. 2024, July–August. "Stop playing favorites." *Harvard Business Review*: 147–151.

UNC Health. 2024. "Who we are." https://www.unchealth.org/about-us/who-we-are

U.S. Census Bureau. 2023 National Population Projections Tables: Main Series. https://www.census.gov/data/tables/2023/demo/popproj/2023-summary-tables.html

Vanderbilt University Medical Center. 2024. "Vanderbilt Medical Center Credo." https://160.129.8.31/wiki/pub/Main/RecognizeReward/vumc-credo.pdf

Uzzi, Brian, and Jarrett Spiro. 2005. "Collaboration and creativity: The small world problem." *American Journal of Sociology* 111 (2): 447–504.

Vanderbilt University Medical Center, 2024. "Vanderbilt Medical Center Credo." https://www.vumc.org/leadership-assembly/our-credo-and-our-promise

Villa, David. 2023, September 28. "The death of brand loyalty." *Forbes.* https://www.forbes.com/sites/forbesagencycouncil/2023/09/28/the-death-of-brand-loyalty/?sh=359eb9c63993

Walmart. 2024, April 30. "Walmart Health is closing." https://corporate.walmart.com/news/2024/04/30/walmart-health-is-closing

Warshawsky, Nora. 2023, June 26. "Investing in nurse leader development: Enhancing efficiency, quality, and financial performance." *Press Ganey Blog.* https://info.pressganey.com/press-ganey-blog-healthcare-experience-insights/investing-in-nurse-leader-development-enhancing-efficiency-quality-financial-performance

Zimlichman, Eyal, and Thomas H. Lee. 2021, May 6. "What went right during the height of Covid-19." *NEJM Catalyst.* https://catalyst.nejm.org/doi/full/10.1056/CAT.21.0176

# *Acknowledgments*

My real introduction to the concepts in this book came in the spring of 2011, when my middle daughter, Sabrina, told me how much she was enjoying one of her college classes. She was learning how people who were socioeconomically disadvantaged tended to have less social capital. They derived less economic benefit from their social networks and were at greater risk for social isolation.

"This sounds something like that book, *Bowling Alone*," I said as we drove along.

"Daddy, you read *Bowling Alone?*" she said, somewhat surprised.

I was a little insulted but had to be honest. "Well," I said, "I bought it when it came out. And I'm sure I read the back cover and some of the introduction. Enough to get the idea."

"Daddy, that's terrible," she said. But after a brief pause, she added, "Actually, it is probably a better use of you to have you buy a lot of books and skim them than having you read every page of a small number of books.

"You are an information broker," she said. "I'm going to give you something for Father's Day that I think you'll like – even if you only read the back cover."

A few weeks later, she gave me a copy of a book from her course – Ronald Burt's *Brokerage and Closure: An Introduction to Social Capital.* As Sabrina might have predicted, I skimmed it at the time, but the challenges of the last several years have made me go back and read every word. The same is true for *Bowling Alone* and the other books I mention in Chapter 1.

I owe a lot to the authors of those books, but I also owe a lot to Sabrina, who pushed me toward them, knowing that I would value their messages. My other two daughters, Simin and Ariana, are both completely tuned into these themes. It's fun to sit with them and my wife Soheyla at meals and kick ideas like these around; we have a whiteboard in our kitchen, and it gets used a lot. I do think of that *Brokerage and Closure* conversation as the moment when I realized that two lines had crossed, and I was now learning more from my children than teaching them.

I also have the good fortune to work for two organizations that are all about building social capital: Press Ganey and *NEJM Catalyst.* I won't list my colleagues in these organizations who have influenced the content of this book here because there are so many of them. Having reflected on what *real* connections are while writing this book, I decided that I would show my gratitude to them individually in other ways.

The same is true for so many good people who work in healthcare organizations that are clients of Press Ganey (past, present, and future) and from the authors of articles that are submitted to *NEJM Catalyst*. These colleagues are responsible for the many examples and case studies included in this book. I feel lucky to have a professional life in which we support people doing this work and get to amplify their impact.

Collectively, working with these colleagues makes me feel rich in social capital – and causes me to want even more.

## About the Author

Thomas H. Lee, MD, is chief medical officer at Press Ganey and a practicing primary care physician and cardiologist at Brigham and Women's Hospital. Before joining Press Ganey in 2013, he was network president of Partners Healthcare System, now known as MassGeneral Brigham. He became a professor at Harvard Medical School and Harvard School of Public Health in 2004. He is editor-in-chief of *NEJM Catalyst* and the author of numerous articles and books, including *Chaos and Organization in Healthcare* (2009), *Eugene Braunwald and the Rise of Modern Medicine* (2013), *An Epidemic of Empathy in Health Care* (2015), *The Good Doctor* (2019), and *Healthcare's Path Forward* (2023).

McChrystal, Stanley, 10, 29–30, 97
Medical University of South
    Carolina (MUSC), coaching
    program, 177
Medicare bundled-payment models,
    VUMC performance
    (maximization), 165–166
Medicare/Medicaid payment rates,
    influence, 151
Medicine, changes, 36–45
Meetings
    family meetings, 74
    formal interactions, 104–105
    group meetings, 74
    notes meeting criteria, 44, 44f
    usage, 99–104
    Zoom meetings, 74
Menino, Tom, 4–5
Meritus Health
    collaborative relationship
    ffps, 87
    huddling culture, 31–32
Metro Nashville Public Schools,
    bundled arrangements, 166
Murthy, Vivek, 6–7
MyHealth Bundles, 166
Mylod, Deirdre, 197

**N**
National Database of Nursing
    Quality Indicators, data
    usage, 186
Natural language processing, usage,
    128, 140
Networks, building, 93, 104
New York University (NYU)
    Langone Health
    communication
    (improvement), ChatGPT
    (usage), 40–45

Note quality standards, compliance
    (audit), 43f
Nurse practitioner, instructions,
    74–75
Nurse rounding frequency, patients
    "recommend the hospital"
    scores (correlation), 76f
NYC Health+Hospitals, wellness
    rooms creation, 84–85

**O**
Obama, Michelle, 5
Obermeyer, Ziad, 62–63
Oklahoma University (OU Health)
    delivery system, 181
One Medical patients (Amazon),
    signup, 153
Online chats, usage, 77
Operational effectiveness, contrast,
    155
Organizational goals, requirement,
    173
Organizational norms, 179
Organizations
    collaboration, 45
    connections, 90–92
    diversity, correlation, 135f
    engagement, drivers, 134–136
    failure, 156
    goals, knowledge, 112–114
    leadership, 111
    missions, 110–111
    money, borrowing, 1
    respect, 140
    social networks, building, 104–106
    values, 110–113
Organization-wide connections
    building, 90
    strengthening, 91
    usage, 91–92

**219**
*Index*